No Brief Candle: Reconceiving Research Libraries for the 21st Century

August 2008

Council on Library and Information Resources

Washington, D.C.

ISBN 978-1-932326-30-7
CLIR Publication No. 142
Published by:

Council on Library and Information Resources
1755 Massachusetts Avenue, NW, Suite 500
Washington, DC 20036
Web site at http://www.clir.org

Additional copies are available for $20 each. Orders must be placed through CLIR's Web site.
This publication is also available online at no charge at http://www.clir.org/pubs/abstract/pub142abst.html.

 The paper in this publication meets the minimum requirements of the American National Standard
for Information Sciences—Permanence of Paper for Printed Library Materials ANSI Z39.48-1984.

Cover image: © 2008 Mary Bono c/o theispot.com

Library of Congress Cataloging-in-Publication Data

No brief candle : reconceiving research libraries for the 21st century.
   p. cm. -- (CLIR publication ; no. 142)
 Papers from a meeting convened by CLIR of librarians, publishers, faculty members, and information technology specialists on
February 27, 2008 in Washington, D.C.
 ISBN 978-1-932326-30-7 (alk. paper)
 1. Research libraries--Congresses. 2. Research methodology--Congresses. 3. Libraries and scholars--Congresses. 4. Research
libraries--Information techonology--Congresses. 5. Library science--Technological innovations. 6. Scholarly publishing--Congresses.
I. Council on Library and Information Resources. II. Title. III. Series.

Z675.R45N53 2008
027.7--dc22

                         2008032646

Contents

Life is no brief candle to me. It is a sort of splendid torch which I have got a hold of for the moment, and I want to make it burn as brightly as possible before handing it onto future generations.

—*George Bernard Shaw*

Foreword

This new title from CLIR, *No Brief Candle: Reconceiving the Research Library for the 21st Century*, is composed of a series of provocative essays, the proceedings of a lively and informed symposium earlier this year in Washington, and a set of recommendations extrapolated from both. While several of the subject headings are familiar—scholarly communication, peer review, preservation of data, and e-science—the conclusions and recommendations are not. The consensus derived from these efforts was unambiguous in calling for more aggressive intervention to better structure and manage the challenges we face.

This report demands change. Common themes include collaboration between librarians, faculty, and information technology experts to articulate strategies and tactical approaches to a rapidly changing environment. This represents a broad research agenda that cannot be executed by a single profession. We are asked collectively to rethink current hiring practices, to provide for new career paths and opportunities for professional development, and to consider redefining libraries as multi-institutional entities. The latter entails a mandate to eliminate redundancy by calibrating resources, staff, and infrastructure functions to the collective enterprise of the federated institutions. This transcends the traditional concept of a library (and by extension a university or college) while preserving the programmatic strengths and mission of the individual schools, and in fact should enhance intellectual productivity in a far more cost-effective fashion.

As the title of this report suggests, this is not a passing phase in higher education. It is a transformational period that requires innovation and risk. I sincerely hope this publication will engender further discussion, new ideas, and collaborative efforts that respect our traditions while recognizing the urgency for invigorated leadership and new direction.

Charles Henry
President
Council on Library and Information Resources

Conference Participants

Charles Henry, *Chair*
President
Council on Library and Information Resources

Fran Blouin
Director, Bentley Historical Library
University of Michigan

Paul Courant
University Librarian and Dean of
    University Libraries
University of Michigan

Andrew Dillon
Dean, School of Information
University of Texas at Austin

David Ferriero
Andrew W. Mellon Director and Chief
    Executive of the Research Libraries
New York Public Library

Amy Friedlander
Director of Programs
Council on Library and Information Resources

Marianne Gaunt
University Librarian
Rutgers University

Suzanne Lodato
Director, Division of Preservation and Access
National Endowment for the Humanities

Richard Luce
Vice Provost and Director of Libraries
Emory University

Stephen G. Nichols
James M. Beall Professor of French
    and Humanities
The Johns Hopkins University

James O'Donnell
Provost
Georgetown University

Jerry Persons
Chief Information Architect
Green Library, Stanford University

Wendy Pradt Lougee
University Librarian
University of Minnesota

Joyce Ray
Associate Deputy Director for Library Services
Institute for Museum and Library Services

Daphnée Rentfrow
Former CLIR Postdoctoral Fellow in the
    Humanities; current MLIS student

Stephen Rhind-Tutt
President
Alexander Street Press

Abby Smith
Consultant

Kathlin Smith
Director of Communications
Council on Library and Information Resources

Donald Waters
Program Officer for Scholarly
    Communications
The Andrew W. Mellon Foundation

Steven Wheatley
Vice President
American Council of Learned Societies

James F. Williams, II
Dean of Libraries
University of Colorado at Boulder

Kate Wittenberg
Manager, Center for Digital Research
    and Scholarship
Columbia University

Karin Wittenborg
University Librarian
University of Virginia

Lee Zia
Program Manager, National Science, Technology,
Engineering and Mathematics Education Digital
    Library Program
National Science Foundation

PART I

A Continuing Discussion on Research Libraries in the 21st Century

Introduction

The information landscape of early twenty-first century higher education is characterized by ubiquitous, digitized, indexed online access to content. Researchers and students begin, and often end, their quest for information online. Results of research can be and increasingly are published without traditional publishers or conventional formats. Access to these results, and to the cultural and scientific record that constitutes the primary resource base for research and teaching, is, however, narrowed by the increasingly exclusive use of licensing instead of selling. This is but one contemporary paradox among many.

What are the critical functions of the research library in this changing landscape? How should we be rethinking the research library in a dynamic, swiftly changing landscape dominated by digital technology? To explore this question, CLIR convened a meeting of librarians, publishers, faculty members, and information technology specialists on February 27, 2008, in Washington, D.C. To prepare for the discussion, CLIR invited eight of the participants to share their perspectives on the future library in brief essays. The essays were circulated before the meeting and are presented in part II of this volume.

Part I of this report begins with an overview and a summary of key meeting themes, or topic threads. The next section summarizes participants' views on what a reconceived research library in the 21st century might look like and what its core functions may be. Next is a discussion of the key challenges to achieving that vision. Part I ends with recommendations to provosts, presidents, deans, faculty members, and library directors about how to realize a reconceived library.

Prologue to a Fundamental Rethinking:
Context and Topic Threads

The breadth of discussion underscored that the future of the research library cannot be considered apart from the future of the academy as a whole. Trends that will influence this future are already evident; foremost among them are a distinct rise in cross-disciplinary research and collaborative projects in the humanities as well as in the sciences, and a concomitant increase in research that involves scholars as well as graduate students and undergraduates.

Researchers are asking new questions and are developing new methodological approaches and intellectual strategies. These methods may entail new models of scholarly communication—for example, a greater reliance on data sets and multimedia presentations. This, in turn, has profound consequences for academic publications: it is difficult to imagine traditional printed books and journals adequately capturing these novel approaches. With the predicted rise in new forms of scholarship, the promotion-and-tenure process, which favors print publications, especially in the humanities, will need to be rethought. As these methods of communication change, the procedures, skills, and expertise that libraries need to manage them will change as well. As cross-disciplinary work increases, it will be necessary to reassess the organization of higher education—its departments, schools, and centers. The research library in the 21st century will thus be profoundly influenced by the transformation of scholarship and research as well as by changes in the traditional organizational structures of a university.

The following topic threads reveal a range of perspectives and questions on the transformation of libraries. Although they are presented as discrete topics, the discussions reflected their interdependence.

Culture of libraries: inhibiting change? Libraries are by nature conserving institutions, and this is what we entrust them to do. But how do we balance a conservative, risk-averse nature with the need to respond to a changing environment? We need to think more deeply about what we want our institutions to conserve. Change will require collective action, and such action will be impossible unless people are closer in spirit with regard to risk. We need to experiment and develop opportunities for work in new sectors or new alignments with different organizations. There is a cost to not taking risk—a danger that libraries will become stuck in a niche that becomes smaller and smaller. As one participant observed, "We could be eradicated in the early stages if we are not a player."

New alliances with students. The Web allows us more autonomy as information creators and consumers. Fewer students today have direct encounters with the library; consequently, they are unaware of a vast amount of useful scholarly information or how to find it.

The library has an opportunity to engage students in new ways—a point that Stephen Nichols explores in his essay "Co-teaching: The Library and Me." The undergraduate population is key to the future working of research library. Faculty members and librarians need to involve undergraduates in using the data sets that are being brought online. Whether exposing students to research materials in the stacks, engaging them in the use of new online data sets, or supporting them in other ways, the library has a potentially huge role in undergraduate and graduate teaching and learning—a function that is tightly aligned with the mission of the university.

Redefining the library workforce. We tend to think of technology as the enabling factor in the new information environment, but the human aspect is just as important. "Technology needs to be addressed as something that enables human abilities for research and learning," observed one participant. People will enable the collaboration with other departments, organizations, and professions that will be critical for the 21st-century library.

With this observation comes a serious challenge: How do we repopulate organizations—universities or libraries—in which half of the workforce will retire in the next decade? Libraries must think about staffing in new ways. Hiring only staff with the master's of library and information science (MLIS) degree is unlikely to bring in the breadth of skill and experience that is needed. Nevertheless, the relative merits of the MLIS should not be our sole focus, cautioned one participant. "We have not been able to translate new ideas, such as co-laboratory or curation, into our normal workflows. We need to think about how we allocate resources. We need to take the expertise we have and think about new positions and new ways to connect with faculty."

We need new career paths for people who want to work in academic libraries, and we need the means to support them. Some libraries use short-term project funding to hire staff with the needed new skills, but find it difficult to retain these talented individuals once a project ends. We also need to accommodate the work styles of a distributed staff. Many who are drawn to work in a library may not wish to be tied to one location. Accommodating a distributed staff would also allow libraries to consider sharing positions with other institutions and to approach certain problems collectively.

New kinds of engagement with faculty. Digital scholarship provides new opportunities for collaboration between faculty and librarians. Libraries have faculty-like expertise that is valuable in many areas of scholarship—for example, in documentary and edition work. Libraries also have great potential to contribute to data curation. At Johns Hopkins University, for example, the library's digital curators create the intellectual data model that enables digital objects to be organized and programmed.

At the same time, libraries will need to become more aware of the data problems within various disciplines and what is being done to solve them. This means, for example, that libraries should be involved in the experimental or developmental stages of such work and should help shape solutions. Extensive work in metadata, for example, is now going on outside of libraries. Libraries would also benefit from greater awareness of the protocol work going on in a

Web-scaled world. "Libraries have often created specialized tools for access to metadata and the associated content, such as Z39.50 and OAI-PMH," noted one participant. "If instead, we always used Web-wide tools and protocols, we could let the Web do what it does best—massive-scale, pervasive tools, just enough complexity to get the job done—while we focus our scarce resources on well-focused, open-sourced, agile, lightweight, loosely coupled services that would make the work of our local communities more efficient and effective."

In the future, data curation will not be static. It will have to encompass the informatics that go into making data accessible in new ways on a continuous basis. It will not mean bringing data to a state of normalcy and then allowing those data to be used. It will require understanding and investing in the research that is going into the use of that data over time. "We need to pay attention to what people have already done because we are going to have to help people use that data in different ways that creators don't care about," said one participant. How will libraries embed themselves on that scale?

Identifying the library's competitive advantage. Several participants noted the keen—almost "Darwinian"—competition for resources within institutions. Can we move from the need to survive to something better? Can we change how we go about our work, rather than just continue to seek more money?

Unless libraries take action, participants cautioned, they risk being left with responsibility for low-margin services that no one else (including the commercial world) wants to provide. An analogy is the U.S. Postal Service (USPS). Its innovative, high-margin services, such as international and overnight delivery, have been taken over by private firms, leaving the USPS largely with its lowest-margin-of-return function: domestic mail delivery. When the broad digital availability of books erodes the comparative advantage of large research collections, where will the library's comparative advantage lie? As Paul Courant notes in his essay "The Future of the Library in the Research University," that advantage could be found in ensuring the "bibliographic" integrity of digital scholarly materials or in developing new tools and services that exploit information technology. During the discussion, he cautioned that in the digital world, universities must think carefully about getting into the business of preserving, migrating, curating, taking care of, and buying more servers for all the world's information, since many of these functions can be outsourced. Two areas in which the library has an interest and can deliver unique value are advocating for preservation and setting standards for quality control. The library should take responsibility for ensuring that mechanisms for preserving digital records exist, and that those mechanisms function as efficiently as possible.

The library's relationship with the commercial sector. There was vigorous debate over the nature of the research library's relationship with commercial entities. Several participants noted that business models and return on investment, rather than the public good, could drive decisions that are at odds with the university's fundamental mission. The library has a "social contract" with the university and cannot abdicate responsibility for basic roles, such as keeping primary data. As an example of what is at stake, one participant noted the closure of the Environmental Protection Agency research libraries under the guise of reorganization. In the wake of the closures, which began in 2006, a significant body of scientific data and information has become unavailable to researchers and the public.

Other participants argued that partnerships with commercial entities will be necessary—and indeed are already common—for libraries. At the very least, libraries will have to "co-evolve" with the parts of the commercial sector that license information so that libraries can ensure ongoing access for scholars. It is also clear that the library community alone does not have the capacity to do software engineering at the level needed in increasingly complex Web environments. Some of the most interesting areas for future library work are being developed by commercial entities. If libraries fail to partner with commercial entities to provide new services, will libraries fall behind and become irrelevant? We must be careful not to focus simply on identifying things libraries do that others don't. University presses made the mistake of attempting to carve out a niche that they alone could fill, and over time this has diminished their function.

There was extensive discussion of the library's relationship with publishers. Libraries must position themselves to retain their intellectual advantage. As one participant noted, "Any functions that don't require human intellect will default to commercial interests."

Expanding the idea of collaboration and collective action. The library's traditional position at the center of campus reflects its function as a crossroads for intellectual activity. Although students, teachers, and researchers increasingly obtain information electronically, the library retains that time-honored position. And in fact, the library's role has become more compelling, given that many of the current challenges in scholarly communication stem from the need to resolve cross-discipline issues in sharing digital resources. Libraries are uniquely situated to work at the nexus of disciplines. But doing this work effectively requires new types of outreach and collaboration. "We need new alignments for moving into new sectors," observed one participant. The definition of "community" must be broadened. Libraries must have the capacity to engage in new ways with the disciplines and to interact more broadly with faculty, publishers, and even commercial interests.[1]

Libraries could play an essential role in helping organize information in such fields as bioinformatics; they could also help create data structures that favor interoperability among disciplines or institutions. Collective action will also be needed to resolve issues relating to copyright law. Sometimes, collaboration makes sense for budgetary reasons—for example, to save money on housing collections through the creation of shared print repositories. In the future,

---

[1] Participants acknowledged that the problem of departmental insularity permeates academic institutions, but that it may be less severe in libraries than it is elsewhere in the academy

the economic viability of libraries is likely to increasingly depend on their ability to forge alliances with the larger community. At the same time, while the potential advantages are numerous, participants acknowledged that there is often a tension between collaboration and self-interest, and that more models for effective collaboration are needed.

Need for experimentation. Participants expressed much enthusiasm about the library as a laboratory—or co-laboratory—for digital scholarship, a theme that Richard Luce explores in his essay "A New Value Equation Challenge: The Emergence of e-Research and Roles for Research Libraries." Increasingly, humanist scholars are creating work with dynamic processes that will need a home. Could the library provide such a home, and might this be a way for librarians to connect with faculty? This would require rethinking how resources are allocated. It can be difficult to convince provosts to hire new staff simply because they are needed for experiments. It can be harder still to sustain momentum and retain innovative staff with short-term project funding. It can also be challenging to bring people together in an organization that doesn't foster innovation. Agreeing to solve collective problems collectively could free up funds for innovation. Can we convince provosts to take a small risk to generate potentially great success?

The fragility of academic publishing. If scholarship is becoming more collaborative in the digital world, at what point is it fixed? Is publication secondary evidence, and is the process somewhere in the middle? What is the role of the commercial publisher in such a scenario? The connection between the university press and the university is fragile. Many publishers are carrying on in old modes; for example, they are focused on converting print to digital. But the potential utility of collections goes beyond just having them in digital form; it extends to the ability to layer intellectual value on top of raw text. We can build new types of research environments with digital publications, and create knowledge that can be reused and reconstituted. Publishers need to add value: the academy demands this. Participants debated whether publishers or academic departments are better positioned to add the intellectual layer even as they acknowledged that publishers, in response to changing markets, seem to be doing this work now. Nevertheless, libraries are moving from being consumers of information to being creators; the research tool Zotero, developed by the Center for History and New Media at George Mason University, is one example.

Related Issues

Peer review. Peer review is fundamental to the advancement of knowledge: it attests to the validity and authority of new thinking within the context of a rich intellectual tradition. But traditional forms of peer review, which have focused exclusively on publication, are no longer sufficient. New models are needed to judge scholarly output that now includes databases, Web sites, and other forms of digital scholarship. Such models might take into account the reception of a work as revealed through citations, links, usage, and commentary on the Web. There is potential value in exposing a work to a much broader and more diverse group of users than would be possible with traditional peer review. (There is also the value of having peers on the Web review a digital resource designed to be shared over the Web.)

At the same time, some participants expressed concern about the risks of interpreting Web hits, rankings, or links as endorsement of quality. Some suggested that peer review on the Web may not reflect serious scholarly values. For example, even a site that is ostensibly peer reviewed, such as Wikipedia, does not source things rigorously. We now have to be able to judge the quality of peer reviewing.

Given the more collaborative nature of digital scholarship, how do we recognize the range of people who are involved in the process of scholarly assurance? Should we, for example, think about extending peer review to the scanner who discovers a miscollated paper? If each contributor to the process is reviewed, the review or quality becomes transparent and builds confidence. More peers will be involved because there is more that needs vetting if things are to be safely transmitted from one community of scholars to another.

Promotion and tenure. Many of the questions relating to promotion and tenure are related to, or extensions of, those relating to peer review. What is the cultural product of a merit society in the 21st century? Is it a traditional journal, or is it a set of processes in social solidarity and knowledge sharing? The traditional efficient, closed system of publications as credentials made promotion-and-tenure decisions clear; it also influenced research funding. In the humanities especially, promotion-and-tenure guidelines are no longer clear-cut. Some institutions now weigh digital scholarship and digital publication more favorably than they used to, but many do not. This inconsistency contributes to the appearance of fragmented, uncoordinated projects in the digital environment and makes it more difficult to bring coherence to electronic resources that preserve and make accessible our cultural heritage. In this way, promotion-and-tenure policies have a direct impact on the quality and utility of digital resources.

International context. Digitization appears to be driving the desire to cooperate abroad. Funding agencies in Europe, for example, want to see partnerships because institutions are often competing for public money. The rationale for collaboration abroad might therefore be viewed as an extension of the rationale for collaboration at home, although rights and regulatory environments are different. Will forging more international collaborations help forge new scholarly relationships as well?

Reconceiving the Library:
A Vision for the 21st Century

Having created a shared context during their initial discussion, participants focused on the following major questions: If we could define and design a library in the 21st century, what would it look like? What would its core functions or role be? What academic mission or parts of academic missions would it support?

The discussion suggested that some core library functions will remain consistent with the library's traditional roles in support of the university's mission and the public good. These roles include preserving, with an emphasis on resolving the challenges of digital preservation and conservation; maintaining special collections and repositories; curation; and teaching research and information-seeking skills. Many believe that these traditional roles have become even more important as the economics of information have changed.

Participants suggested that the library of the 21st century will be more of an abstraction than a traditional presence. Rather than reaching a consensus on the future, participants offered a range of perspectives:

- The 21st-century library will mirror basic changes in how scholars work and will evolve in step with new scholarly methodologies and the scholarly environment. Working at the nexus of disciplines and across boundaries, libraries will have the flexibility, expertise, and organizational capacity needed to be partners in research involving large, heterogeneous data sets. The library will not necessarily be a physical space, and it may not be a collection. It might take the form of a distributed project.
- The library's work will be organized according to the interests of a broader number of stakeholders. It will depend on mechanisms that ensure the quality of digital resources and make it possible to share them. The new library will be organized to work collectively on common problems; this may include federating collections or staff or coordinating collection management decisions. For example, libraries will routinely make decisions about keeping print and digital resources so that each institution does not have to retain everything.
- The library will exploit the potential of embeddability, enabling users to interact with information at progressive levels of value-added functionality—from a simple link, to automated metadata harvesting, to "actionable" data.
- The library will be a laboratory for understanding how a new generation of faculty and students do their work, and for supporting experimentation and innovation in processes that enhance e-research across many communities.
- Librarians will have deep experience in intellectual problems such as the structure and construct of information, the delivery of information, and the specialized needs of information communities. Institutions will share expertise.

- The library will play a critical role in ensuring the authentication and persistence of digital information, including Web-based information, that is important to future scholars.
- Library staff will be more distributed than at present. Librarians might do some of their work in spaces that are traditionally academic spaces, and faculty might use wired or smart classrooms in the library.

One participant suggested re-envisioning the library by turning the organization inside out.[2] Look at where the fringe activity is now, he said, and think about how it would look at the center of library functions. At the center could be investment in metadata—making material available to the scholarly community in a systematic way. Activities such as management of print archives and rationalizing print collections are at the periphery now. What if they were at the center? Multimedia collections are relatively weak, as is the ability to describe them. Suppose they were at the center? Scholarly communication and the creation of digital resources would be put at the center. Print and journal material, now central, would be at the edges.

Challenges And Constraints

What will it take to realize the vision of the next library? Meeting participants discussed the need for a new service paradigm that supports roles rather than functions, and process rather than product. Professional communities—librarians, faculty members, publishers, technical staff—must be less insular. The importance of engendering collaboration, and the difficulty in doing so, figured prominently in the discussion as well as in the essays. Implicit in the discussions was the fundamental challenge of how long it takes to effect change. Participants noted several challenges raised in the earlier discussion:

- Libraries tend to be risk-averse organizations; to remain relevant, they must be willing to experiment and innovate.
- A sense of ownership—for example, of staff or collections—has kept libraries from engaging in truly collective work. Among faculty, competition for grants often induces self-interested behaviors, rather than collaboration.
- Adherence to traditional hiring practices, including, in some cases, restricting hiring to individuals with the MLIS degree, makes it difficult for libraries to attract or retain staff with special expertise, such as a disciplinary background to connect teaching, research, and collections.
- Half of today's librarians will retire in the next decade. We need new career paths for people who want to work in academic libraries, and we need the means to support them.
- Experimental or innovative projects are frequently supported by special grants. Libraries invest significant time and training

---

[2] This idea was initially raised in spring 2007 at a meeting of associate university librarians at The Andrew W. Mellon Foundation.

in special project staff, but have trouble retaining them once the grant ends.

- At this time, we do not know who will be responsible for analyzing and interpreting various kinds of dynamic information resources and making them available to the public. If this responsibility falls to the academy, how will the library address it?
- Production of data and metadata on a very large scale for broad use needs a high level of organization. We do not have institutions that can deliver that organization.
- The traditional separation between libraries and commercial entities needs to be reconsidered. There is enormous potential in productive collaboration between libraries and for-profit corporations.
- As more information is digitized, print repositories will become increasingly important. We are currently stymied by the lack of effective print repositories and models for organizing them.
- Libraries' ability to share digital information and keep it usable is limited by a range of issues relating to copyright.

Recommendations

Transformations in scholarly communication and in the organization of higher education will demand new ways of doing business—not only within the library but throughout the academy as well. Research libraries will need broad institutional support as they seek to meet the demands of this new environment. On the basis of the discussion and the essays, CLIR proposes the following recommendations for higher education leadership.

1. In collaboration with library professionals, professors, and information technologists, administrators in higher education need to develop a rigorous research agenda that will explore the influences that are transforming education so that they may better respond to and manage change.

2. The research library should be redefined as a multi-institutional entity. The current model of the library as a stand-alone service provider to the university is obsolescent. Exploiting digital networks and emerging digital libraries and research environments, many libraries should deaccession duplicate copies of printed books, form coalitions that minimize costs for collection development, and consider sharing staff on a consortial, federated basis. Collaboration can generate savings that the library can allocate to other activities supporting teaching and research.

3. Collaboration should undergird all strategic developments of the university, especially at the service function level. Greater collaboration among librarians, information technology specialists, and faculty on research project design and execution should be strongly supported. Areas of immediate concern include mecha-

nisms of scholarly publishing, institutional repository development and sustainability, data curation broadly defined, and digital resource development. Any research project, digital resource, or tool that cannot be shared, is not interoperable, or otherwise cannot contribute to the wider academic and public good should not be funded.

4. Institutions need to support environments, within and external to libraries, that not only promote but demand change. More funds should be allocated for experimental projects and new approaches; staff with nontraditional or new areas of expertise must be hired.

5. Higher education communities, working with research libraries, need to define what models of scholarly communication represent a valid cultural product. Currently, the printed book and journal article take precedence, but the digital environment entails a more nuanced understanding of scholarship as a process in social solidarity and sharing of information. Criteria for promotion and tenure need to be reassessed. Finally, peer review requires similar study. It may prove essential for all aspects of the scholarly process—data sets, research background, Web commentaries, links, and other manifestations of the digital age that are made available and sustained over time.

6. Instruction and delivery mechanisms should be designed according to what we know of human learning and discovery. The functions of libraries must be aligned with the core mission of research and education at the institutional level. We need to create professional and practice layers that enhance research and teaching across disciplines.

7. University administrators and librarians should consider creating new training and career paths for professionals going into the area of scholarly communication. New leadership programs need to be developed that reflect the rise in collaborative research and that integrate support services such as those provided by research libraries into the process and methodologies of research.

8. Institutions should use studio and design experiences as the basis of a new library school curriculum. Students of library and information sciences should learn to participate in the design and delivery of information resources that serve the scholarly community. Academic librarians should be engaged in the process through project provision and supervision.

9. Higher education needs to articulate not only the benefits it conveys to university and college students but also the value it provides to the public. The popular conception of higher education has been influenced by critics who dismiss its perceived high

costs and the impracticality of its curriculum, by those who are intent on taxing the larger endowments, and by those who want federal intervention to lower tuition costs. The cultural, social, and technological advancements that higher education can foster are lost in this impassioned rhetoric.

PART II

The Research Library in the 21st Century: Collecting, Preserving, and Making Accessible Resources for Scholarship

Abby Smith

Collecting, Preserving, Making Accessible: Where We Come From

According to Samuel Johnson, "Knowledge is of two kinds. We know a subject ourselves, or we know where we can find information upon it." Until recently, we knew where we could find information upon any given subject—in a research library. Libraries collected, preserved, and made available an array of resources needed by scholars. The bigger and more comprehensive the research library, the greater was the community's access to knowledge, as well as access to those experts who could help patrons navigate the library's geography of knowledge. Because scholarship has been primarily print and artifact based, the library was bound to acquire and then maintain in usable form scholarly literature and primary resources in order to make them accessible. In hindsight, it seems unlikely that between them, so many libraries would have redundantly purchased so much of the non-unique secondary scholarly literature if they could have made it accessible to their patrons in less expensive ways—ways that did not demand large and continuing investments in physical, technical, and staff infrastructure. The success of interlibrary loan gives some evidence to this surmise.

Whereas libraries once seemed like the best answer to the question "Where do I find. . . ?" the search engine now rules. Researchers—be they senior scholars or freshmen—no longer make the library the first stop in their search for knowledge. The shift from producing and consuming information in hard copy to multimedia digital form has moved the center of information gravity from research libraries to the Internet, and done so in a dramatically brief period. The preconditions for this sudden shift were laid in the 19th century by the development of audio and visual formats—still and moving images, recorded sound, and, ultimately, formats combining

Abby Smith is an independent consultant. She was formerly Director of Programs at the Council on Library and Information Resources.

sound and image. A bifurcation eventually emerged between campus-based "general collection" libraries, which focused on secondary literature and a highly selective group of primary sources (both print and nonprint), and libraries not serving first and foremost a faculty and student body, and which focused on "special collections."[1]

I mention this division of labor among research libraries because it is a mistake to grant exclusive agency to digital information in the shift away from the centrality of academic research libraries in collecting and preserving resources for scholarship. The academic research library has been predominant in collecting and preserving text-based scholarly literature, but it has not been the primary home for statistical data, cartographic materials, manuscript collections, prints and photographs, film, broadcast television and radio, folklore documentation, natural history specimens, and an overwhelming preponderance of primary source materials needed by scholars in the humanities, social sciences, and physical sciences. The challenges facing academic research libraries are fundamentally different from those facing nonacademic research libraries, not because of their mission (they both serve scholarship) but because of their user base. I will focus my remarks on the former because they are facing more urgent pressures to change, and so emerging trends for research libraries of all stripes may be easier to comprehend.

If we take libraries-as-first-resort in search out of the equation, what is left looks something like stewardship, loosely defined: ensuring long-term access to content in reliable, secure, and authentic form. But we already know that a significant portion of digital scholarly literature and primary resources—that is, the portion available through licensed agreements—is seldom in the possession and care of research libraries. Perhaps a preliminary answer to the question "What are the core functions of the research library with respect to collecting, preserving, and making accessible resources for scholarship?" might be that research libraries will be stewards of some sectors of the information universe, but they will not be the same sectors as before. So which sectors will they be?

Collecting, Preserving, Making Accessible: Where We Are Headed

To answer that question, we will examine six trends in the academic research environment that are likely to shape scholarship in the next decades. From these trends we may learn something about what resources scholars will use and how. First, however, I believe that one thing about scholarship will never change: scholars will demand access to information resources to examine what others have discovered and thought; to use and reuse evidence and scientific conclusions; and to publish results of their own research based on these resources. That is why their sources must be authentic, reliable, easy to find and retrieve, and easy to use and reuse.

---

[1] Separately incorporated "special format" libraries on campus share features with both types of libraries; how much varies greatly depending on how closely each is integrated with and funded by the main university library.

1. Ascendance of science

The physical and life sciences are expanding their footprint on almost every Research I university campus. Science programs have become huge cost centers, consuming an ever-larger portion of university expenditures on research infrastructure. Because of the way science is funded, however, these programs are often viewed on campus as revenue centers: they are recipients of the largest federal grants and the largest philanthropic donations, in the tens and hundreds of millions of dollars. Science is where the big donors like to make their mark, comparable to the way that libraries were magnets for philanthropic donations in the 19th and 20th centuries. So science, which costs universities a great deal, will nonetheless increase in charisma; and the humanities, which neither cost so much nor bring in so much money, appear at present to be politically disadvantaged.

But that is just the money side of the equation. More significant in the long run is the influence of scientific reasoning on nonscientific domains of research. There is a general expansion of quantitative reasoning and methods into normally qualitative disciplines. For example, imaginative uses of geographic information systems (GIS) in history, archaeology, and art history, and data mining in classics and other text-driven disciplines are breathing new life into old disciplines. There is a burgeoning demand among social scientists to incorporate into their research an array of scientific data—such as epidemiological information and distribution patterns of genetic variations with health care statistics—and methods, such as GIS-based geographical analysis used to plot and examine polling or census data, consumption patterns, and so forth.

Finally, more and more scientists are recognizing that persistent data management is crucial to their research. Hence, they are developing library-like centers for the collection, curation, preservation, and access of data. The National Science Foundation has encouraged them to do so by putting out a call to develop such structures as key components of scientific cyberinfrastructure. Private foundations, including the Alfred P. Sloan and the Gordon and Betty Moore Foundations, are making equally significant investments in scholarly communication that include stewardship as well as dissemination.

2. Development of digital humanities

The accelerated development of digital humanities is an even more significant trend for research libraries, if only because humanists have been their primary clientele. Beyond the increasing use of quantitative research methods in the humanities, there is a growing demand by humanists to access and manipulate resources in digital form. With the primacy of "data-driven humanities," certain humanities disciplines will eventually grow their own domain-specific information specialists. While perhaps trained as librarians or archivists, such specialists will work embedded in a department or disciplinary research center.

Of greater import is the emergence of digital humanists who continue to focus on narrative, discursive, and essentially qualitative ways of investigating what it means to be human. It is these scholars, interrogating new forms of discourse, narrative, communication, community building, and social networking, who will spend most of their time on the open Web and use wiki and blogging applications, social software, and other as-yet-undreamt-of applications. All these multimedia forms of discourse will present special challenges for collection development and preservation because of their inherent bias toward process over product, a bias that resists fixing expression in the canonical forms upon which analog preservation practices are dependent.

3. Emphasis on process over product (with respect to scholarly communication)

Distinctions between formal, archival publication and informal modes of scholarly communication are becoming nebulous. Among scientists, we have seen for more than a decade a preference for various types of informal, preprint-type sharing of working drafts, an informal mode of communication that has greater impact on the development of scholarship than the final, archival or formal publication does. (The latter, however, will probably continue to have a greater impact on scholarly careers, at least for the short term.) Humanists are also becoming more engaged with informal, narrative forms of communication, with graduate students and tenured professors alike using vernacular social software applications to build communities of discourse.

What does this mean for scholarly communication? I recently heard a tenured literary theorist say that she hoped never to publish a monograph again. When she gives talks, they are immediately blogged, and she finds this mode of discourse with other scholars highly productive and immediately gratifying. It has also reframed her view of the timetable of monograph production, shifting from inevitable-if-slow to arbitrary-and-obsolete. So much for the time-honored notion that humanists are immune to the pressure of time to get out their research results!

Finally, in many domains we see an erosion of the traditional distinctions between primary and secondary sources and flows of information. Many scholars now argue that publication and dissemination can and should represent evidence as well as argument, and that is precisely what they demand of new-model scholarly communication.

4. Mobile and ubiquitous computing

The headline here is that the laptop is the library. It was recently reported that a researcher at IBM is working on a storage technology that will allow an entire college library to be stored on mobile devices as small as the current iPod.2 Whether it happens two years or five years hence, whether it is IBM or some other company that realizes this goal, the handheld library is foreordained. Even without such a device in hand, we see the dominance of consumer technologies and applications, both commercial and free, in the academy. It is not only the undergraduates who arrive on campus with iPods that can stream courseware and the senior faculty who consult just-in-time Web-based references, even offline, through Zotero. It is that undergraduates can have a sophisticated command of geospatial thinking simply by opening up Google Earth; they do not have to master the intricacies of GIS available through expensive ESRI applications. It also means that graduate students do not require a high-quality but expensive (and far from ubiquitous) resource like ARTstor for creating presentations, sharing links, and drafting articles, when an astounding number of equally high-quality images are available free on Flickr. Then the question for research libraries becomes how to provide persistent access to these sources. Or does it? Does that become someone else's responsibility?

5. Data deluge

Given the scale of information that scholars must cope with daily, opportunities to acquire skills in information management should be a key element of their education and training. The goal of professional training as a scholar is to maximize the autonomy and enhance the creativity of the scholar as an arbiter of information. We should never underestimate how carefully successful scholars manage their time; ready access to information that fits within the time frames set by the scholar is often the most important criterion in information seeking. Only some aspects of scholarship demand information meeting the rarefied benchmarks of reliability, authenticity, and persistence. That is why many scholars begin searching for information on the Web, and why they often turn to Amazon.com, not their local OPAC, to do a "quick and dirty" literature search.

With one more stage of breakthrough in storage, we could see significant change in the way individuals are able to manage the data deluge. The device under development at IBM, mentioned previously, "could begin to replace flash memory in three to five years, scientists say. Not only would it allow every consumer to carry data equivalent to a college library on small portable devices, but a tenfold or hundredfold increase in memory would be disruptive enough to existing storage technologies that it would undoubtedly unleash the creativity of engineers who would develop totally new entertainment, communication and information products."3

---

2 John Markoff. 2007. "Redefining the Architecture of Memory." *The New York Times* (September 11). Available at http://www.nytimes.com/2007/09/11/ technology/11storage.html?_r=1&oref=slogin (accessed November 24, 2007).
3 Ibid.

6. Rising costs and changing funding models for higher education

Competition for funding among all units on campus means that the library must continuously demonstrate its value; it must also bring in money or lower costs simply to provide services demanded by their users. Given the financial pressures on all aspects of higher education, it is imperative to change the service model of the library. When the world was smaller, libraries strove to be many things to many different constituents. The library must now focus on specific communities. Its role in pedagogy seems clear, as pedagogy is always locally based. But an individual library's role in research, an increasingly global enterprise, is not so clear. Each research library will need to find its niche. This is why the "special-collection" research libraries that have a tradition of being subject or format based may, in the long term, be better models for research libraries than campus-based general-collection libraries are.

Collecting, Preserving, Making Accessible: Two Roles for the Library

So what can we infer from these six trends for the research library with respect to scholarly resources? First, let us define the research library as a line item in a university budget dedicated to managing information resources for research and teaching.[4] For our purposes, it matters little whether in 25 years that function will be performed by something with the discrete name of "library." Whatever its name, that entity will need to focus clearly on two specific roles: one local, the other networked and part of a national and transnational research cyberinfrastructure.

In its local role, the library will be optimized to meet the needs of its campus community. The library is likely to provide repository infrastructure for stewardship of university-based information assets. Most of those assets will support pedagogy, administration, student life, alumni affairs, and other things vital to the school. A much smaller portion of them will support research. Research will be a far more global phenomenon than local institutions can support on their own.

In its networked role, the library will be able to support research and dissemination to the extent that it is tightly networked into the increasing cluster of inter-institutional collaborations that enable the creation and use of scholarly content. These collaborations will be key elements of research cyberinfrastructure, an infrastructure that will be a research-and-dissemination platform. In the magic phrase of the digital era, it "will scale," be ubiquitous, and support a variety of scholarly domains, from astronomy to nanobiology, archaeology to urban design. The next-generation research library must be firmly

---

4 A characterization recently used by Kimberly Douglas, university librarian at Caltech, that distills the relationship of the library to a community of scholars and why it can command so much university money.

embedded in that infrastructure, because that will be the platform to which scholars will gain access on their laptop library.

The exact models of stewardship and dissemination in the cyber-infrastructure will be determined by the evolution of domain practices. In the quantitative fields, we see domain-specific stewardship models such as genome and protein databases, the Virtual Observatory, and the Inter-university Consortium for Political and Social Research (ICPSR), among others, that look quite similar to "special-collection" libraries writ large. These entities are scaled to collect, preserve, and make accessible digital research content. They are deeply embedded within the communities of researchers that they serve. These stewardship models are optimized to handle content created by and for the academic community.

These networked efforts should also be extended to the data that are created outside the dominion of the academy, of particular value to humanists. This content comes in roughly two flavors—commercially created (usually gated) and publicly networked (ungated). So far, one organization focusing on stewardship of publicly networked content—the Internet Archive—has achieved scale. It is so successful at this that it provides vital services for numerous national libraries and government organizations seeking to archive their domains. Scarcely a decade old, it is already indispensable. While scores of university research libraries are collecting Web-based content in selected areas, none of them achieves, or even aims for, the scale or breadth necessary to collect digital content that scholars will demand. While I believe that certain research libraries can achieve comparable scale in collecting, it is unclear that any are planning to do so, or that they even see this as part of their core mission. It is equally unclear which libraries, if any, other than the Library of Congress, are contemplating large-scale partnerships with commercial content providers to ensure long-term access to primary digital resources. This is bad news. In the absence of such efforts, researchers will be forced to rely on commercial entities to preserve and make accessible their own content on their own terms.

Where academic libraries have been more effective, not surprisingly, is in joining networked efforts, such as LOCKSS, CLOCKSS, and Portico, to ensure persistent access to scholarly literature. These are important efforts and have much to teach about the challenges of forging long-term trusted relationships that can ensure access to content over time. For this is the make-it-or-break-it challenge for academic and nonacademic research libraries alike: to forge close working relationships with content providers—be they individuals, for-profit corporations, or learned societies—to ensure persistent access to that content for generations to come.

Conclusion

Research libraries evolved over the course of centuries to solve the problem of providing access to information. The library was the place where the artifacts of knowledge were aggregated and individuals came to consult them. The stewardship of artifacts will continue to be a collective responsibility of the research library community. As more of their content becomes available through digital surrogates, more opportunities will open for libraries to design a collective solution to preserving the artifacts.

But if we were to design a system to address the needs of digital scholarly resources, it would certainly be different from the library. The system would combine the functions of library, information technology, and scholarly publishing. Those who manage information resources for research and teaching would take it as ground truth that research is a global and distributed phenomenon. So, too, should be the infrastructure that undergirds it. These managers—be they called librarians or not—would be responsible for building and maintaining the multiple partnerships with scholars, learned societies, content creators, publishers, and, above all, with each other across the globe, that would support persistent access to high-quality research resources.

The Future of the Library in the Research University

*Paul N. Courant**

I have been asked to write about the role and functions of research libraries in the 21st century, informed by three perspectives that combine quite naturally for me: those of a former provost, an economist, and a library director. The principle that unites these perspectives, at least in my mind, is the economic idea of a "public good." Where economists may be fairly or unfairly thought of as bean counters who care only about the bottom line, the field of public economics, which I have been practicing for several decades, is largely concerned with the production of goods and services whose value is best realized through collective action, rather than in the marketplace. Universities, the practice of scholarship, and libraries all fall within this category.

The key feature of public goods is that their consumption is non-rival, meaning that the cost of adding users is zero. National defense, the brightness of the sun, the view of a distant mountain range, access to a catalog record available on WorldCat, and information generally are public goods in this sense. Markets are not effective at producing the optimal amount of such goods, because it is inefficient to exclude people if the cost of adding them is zero, but charging a price of zero will not cover the fixed costs of producing the good. Thus, production of public goods is generally left to public institutions, and the mechanisms for determining the best amount to produce are political as well as economic.

The fact that markets are not good at producing public goods, including those produced by the university library, does not imply that economic considerations of cost, technology, and demand are irrelevant. On the contrary, where markets cannot be relied upon to pro-

Paul N. Courant is University Librarian and Dean of Libraries, Harold T. Shapiro Collegiate Professor of Public Policy, and Arthur F. Thurnau Professor of Economics and of Information at the University of Michigan.

* I am grateful to Matthew Nielsen for excellent research assistance and even better conversations and comments.

duce things of value, the job of determining how and how much to produce is that much more difficult; this is the subject matter of public economics. Our task requires knowledge of the library's purposes, the technologies that can be deployed to accomplish those purposes, and the cost and effectiveness of deploying alternative technologies. Recent and foreseeable changes in information technology are especially interesting in this context because they make possible new and different ways of organizing, finding, and publishing (in the broad sense of making public) scholarship both old and new. Whoever are the actors (and most faculty, provosts, and librarians may well lead long and productive lives without developing more than a nodding acquaintance with any economist), the problems that the research library faces in responding to changes in information technology are very much within the purview of economics.

The provost's job is to articulate the demand for the library's collections and services. The provost must ensure that the library is delivering value for the institution in which the library sits, and must continually assert the primacy of scholarship and academic work, including teaching, in the library's mission. Thus, the provost identifies the library's objectives in the context of all of the university's missions.[1] The provost also helps define and implement the business model(s) that sustain(s) the library, especially the revenue side. The provost is similarly responsible for the efficient production of many other public goods within the university.

Although I cannot speak for provosts in general, my experience as the provost of a major research university persuades me that the quality (both academic and in the marketplace) of undergraduate education is vital to the continued success of the great research universities. This observation has important consequences for how we think about the future of research libraries that are embedded in universities. Thus, although the assigned topic of this essay is the future of research libraries, my subject will be both narrower and broader— namely, libraries in research universities. Such libraries, with their universities, cannot limit their purview to research, although I will argue that their signal contribution to undergraduate education is the teaching of scholarly methods.

The library director—the position that I currently hold but know least well of the three—helps the provost determine the library's missions and the mechanisms that the library can employ to greatest effect in service of those missions. (Of course, the director also does a fair amount of the heavy lifting in seeing to it that the work is done.) The director brings to bear the expertise of the librarians as well as perspectives on both scholarship and education that derive from the rich interactions among the library, faculty, and students. Libraries and librarians know a great deal that is crucial to the effective func-

---

[1] Eleanor Jo Rodger makes a brief and persuasive argument that in order to succeed, libraries must deliver value to their "host systems." Adapting her nomenclature, in this essay the university is by far the most important part of the host system, and the provost is its agent. See Rodger, E. J. 2007. What's a Library Worth? *American Libraries* 38(8): 58-60.

tioning of academic institutions. When things are working well, this knowledge is shared at many levels, including the reference desk (or the reference IM site) and conversations between subject specialists and faculties. It is the director's job to ensure that the expertise of librarians and other library staff is developed and deployed to maximum effect. As the technology and associated social and political structures that affect academic work and research libraries continue to change, a vital part of the library's role is to keep up with the changes and to develop and deliver an array of tools, services, and ideas that help students and faculty do their work.

With public goods as well as private ones, much of what is at stake can be reduced to demand and supply. In the public goods case, the determination of demand is the more difficult problem. Taking into consideration technology, publishing, the rights environment, the state of current collections, and the cost of adding to those collections and maintaining them in any number of possible configurations, what do we want the library to do?

The Library as Intermediate Good

The library provides essential infrastructure—largely in the form of reliable and well-documented access to prior scholarship, data, the cultural record, and other research materials—that is necessary to the effective practice of scholarship. It is worth noting that this description of the mission of the library is robust with respect to history, organization, and technical change. Providing the infrastructure of scholarly work was the library's mission before the invention of the printing press, and continues to be the library's mission in a world where making public materials that are used in scholarship is accomplished in myriad media, many of them digital (making content easy to copy and to transmit, at least technically).

The library's value is derived from the requirement that scholars, teachers, and students have easy, rapid, reliable, and documented access to the rich set of materials that constitute the scholarly and cultural record. If some other institution were to provide the same or essentially similar access to those materials, the university library would have no clear mission. What matters is that the academic work be done, and be done well. The library's future depends on its effectiveness in delivering materials and expertise requisite for excellent academic work.

Libraries should also be efficient, in the sense that they should deliver the services they provide at as low a cost as possible. Of course, for many services the library provides, the lowest possible cost is not low. (The same applies to much in the research university.) Work that requires individual attention by highly skilled academics does not, and cannot, come cheap. Academics and academic librarians will sometimes argue that our calling is so exalted that it would be wrong even to think about cost.[2] This is nonsense. Precisely be-

---

[2] Consider, for example, the assertion that "cataloging is a public good which should be supported regardless of economic concerns." (Fallgren, N. J. 2007. Brief meeting summary: May 9, 2007—Structures and standards for bibliographic data. Accessed December 3, 2007, from http://www.loc.gov/bibliographic-future/meetings/meetingsummary-may9.html.)

cause academic work is so valuable, we should attend to cost all the time. If we do not, we will waste resources that we could have been using to advance scholarly work. It is not helpful to assert that the library should be great no matter what the cost.

Harold Shapiro once wrote that a competent faculty and administration will always see important things to do whose costs greatly exceed the resources available.[3] If research universities and their libraries were ever at a loss for things to spend more money on, we would either have (a) solved all the world's problems or (b) used up all our ideas, and hence should give way to someone else. Neither circumstance looks likely. I am not saying that the university library should be a profit-oriented business, or that we should count beans and base our decisions solely on the sorts of things that accountants or librarians are good at counting. But I am saying that we should always be looking for ways to do what we do more cheaply as well as better, because if we can do some things more cheaply (holding quality constant) it enables us to do everything better, including improving quality.

Some Economics of University Libraries and Academic Publishing

Historically, the university library has met the definition of a public good with respect to its own campus. For the population associated with the university, and geographically nearby, the collections could be made almost freely accessible with little or no effect of adding to the population. Going back to the definition of public goods developed above, use of library materials on campus is very close to being nonrival. (Textbooks and assigned work in large courses are the exception that proves the rule, here, and with respect to those materials, the academic library acts very much like a public library.) In the larger economy of higher education, however, the quality of the library was, and still is, of significant consequence, because the better the library, the higher the quality of faculty and students that can be attracted to the university, and the higher the quality of research that can be undertaken there. Both reputation and economic resources depend on academic quality, and the library is a vital intermediate good in any university's ability to produce academic quality.

When almost all resources were in print, the economist, the provost, and the librarian were in sync, although the librarian might have been a little less concerned with cost than the others. By improving the library, one could improve the competitive position of the particular university relative to other universities. Distinguished departments were built around distinguished collections. An excellent collection at some distance was not a substitute for an excellent collection at one's home institution. Hence, the payoff to investing in excellent collections at home was clear to all. To be sure, Interlibrary

3 Shapiro, Harold T. 1987. *Tradition and Change: Perspectives on Education and Public Policy*. Ann Arbor: University of Michigan Press, p. 139.

Loan makes it possible for scholars who are not proximate to excellent collections to do their work, but there is a significant difference between having essentially instantaneous access and access that is removed in both time and space. Thus, marketlike competition among the great research institutions provided a mechanism for supporting a system of superb research libraries.

The world of print also used a complementary set of technologies that supported the publishing industry. Printing, paper, and binding are expensive. Making print copies is expensive. There are substantial scale economies with respect to the size of a print run. Before undertaking the investment required to publish several thousand copies of a monograph (the high end for scholarly work even in the good old days), the publisher would want assurances that there was a market for the work. So the publisher would take steps to have it carefully vetted by experts in the field—the very sorts of people who would buy it and ask their libraries to buy it—and edited by people who were good at making the product attractive and usable, the better to sell more copies.

The interests of universities and academic publishers meshed well. To be sure, the publishers would have been even happier without the doctrine of first sale, but basically, they produced for our libraries, using the talents of our faculty, and we were able to take their editorial behavior as a strong indicator of the academic value of the work. Articles in refereed journals or monographs of established presses were just the ones we wanted, and libraries bought them, took care of them, and made them (approximately) permanently available to our campuses. If we had lots of them, we could support scholarship of great breadth and depth, so we have the great universities attached to their great libraries, and tenure cases being decided based on the peer review of the people who created and used the works that filled those libraries. As a bonus, because most works were collected by several libraries, copies could be compared, albeit at some expense, for authenticity and consistency.

In the digital world, the technological underpinnings of this economy—expensive print and expensive distribution (hence an advantage to local access, replicated across institutions) disappear. With digital production of text and images, making copies of things is essentially free (in one form) and getting cheap (print-on-demand), even in the traditional book. It's still very expensive to produce a beautiful book, but now it's quite cheap to produce a pretty nice book, and essentially free to distribute a usable digital file, and for many purposes the cheap and free alternatives perform adequately or better than the costly options. So, much of the academic work of the present and the future exhibits the character of a public good—once produced (and, of course, the initial production is still not cheap, but those costs are borne almost entirely by academic institutions and granting agencies) the work can be distributed to all who wish to see it at essentially no cost. It is possible to exclude users, of course, and under current law and custom, exclusion is straightforward. But exclusion under current technology is plainly inefficient and difficult to sustain, especially when authors, at least in many fields, cheerfully post their stuff on the Web where anyone can find it, legally or not.

Publishing, academic libraries, and the particulars of peer review were all developed in a world where printing, copying, and distributing were expensive. We no longer live in that world. How then, should we configure the library—and publishing and peer review—to take full advantage of the change?

The Future of Libraries in Research Universities

Research universities continue to require easy and quick access to reliable and replicable scholarly resources. Essentially all of the scientific journal literature is now distributed electronically, and most of the rest of the journal literature will follow shortly. Digital distribution has been relatively unimportant for monographs, but they, too, are basically born digital, and in the fairly near future one expects that the technical problems of e-books will be solved, although I would not be surprised if inexpensive print-on-demand is an important part of the solution for quite some time. Meanwhile, many great print collections are being digitized. It is likely that almost all of the scholarly literature will be available in digital form, at least somewhere, within the next 10 years or so.

The implications for the cost of library storage are potentially huge. One can imagine that new work will take up relatively little space, and that a substantial part of the existing monographic literature can be moved off site and replaced for most purposes with electronic files. (This will require that reasonable arrangements can be made with holders of rights who can be found easily, with reasonable statutory arrangements made for the cases where rights holders are hard to find. There would be enormous gains relative to the status quo for both users and rights holders, so the economist in me believes that such arrangements should be relatively easy to make.) Thus the library's ever-growing claim on space would attenuate, affording, among other things, the opportunity to provide both services and improved access to scholarly materials that are currently stored securely but inaccessibly.

Before most humanities faculty—and, hence, their libraries and provosts—would be willing to substitute electronic copies of print works for the originals, they would have to be assured permanent access to the originals. This could most effectively be accomplished through a small number of print repositories, with very good security, climate control, and the like, with costs and access shared across a network of libraries. I expect to see an interesting tension for provosts, librarians, and other academic leaders as they begin to move in this direction. On the one hand, the availability of shared and sharable depositories will tend to erode the competitive advantage that the most prestigious libraries derive from the size of their local collections. On the other hand, it is precisely those libraries that will stand to save the most from using collective repositories and that have the most special collections materials that could be used more effectively in liberated local space. Moreover, the most prestigious institutions will have the greatest demand for developing new tools and services that exploit information technology. If the library continues to be the source of local expertise and innovation in both services and collection development, investments in the library will continue to generate competitive advantage for their institutions, although some collection development, notably the collection of audio and video clips, Web pages, Flickr sites, and the like, would benefit greatly from coordinated strategies across institutions.

Bibliographic reliability is much more difficult to guarantee in a digital world than in the world of print, and will require a set of social institutions that can identify and assure the stability of copies of record. Portico and LOCKSS have developed mechanisms to deal with this for a subset of the journal literature. It remains to be seen if their efforts are sufficiently comprehensive and trusted. I believe that the leadership of the great universities will have to create a collective institution whose job it will be to assure the "bibliographic" integrity of digital scholarly materials. I can't imagine anyone but librarians in charge of these institutions if they are to succeed. The level of inter-university cooperation required for this to work is unprecedented, as is the level of cooperation required for the shared print repositories outlined in the previous paragraph. As is often the case, the technical requirements are easier to attain than the social and institutional arrangements that are necessary to take full advantage of technical change.

The library will succeed (because it will have plenty of valuable work to do) if it continues to be the locus of expertise and innovation regarding scholarly information, how to find it, and how to use it.

Near the beginning of this essay, I suggested that effective undergraduate education would be essential to the success of research universities, and that the teaching of scholarly method is the most important aspect of undergraduate education.[4] Our students must learn how to make judgments about the quality of information that they use. I do not presume that things in libraries are "good" and that things on the open Web are not good. Rather, I argue that it is essential that students be able to check on facts and assertions using reliably replicable sources. Libraries provide the infrastructure for this kind of teaching just as they do for scholarship, as the methods involved are the same in both. Success here will require two things: (1) coordinated curricula in which librarians and faculty demand the engaged use of library materials and library expertise; and (2) the ability to search library collections with something like the same ease and efficacy with which one can search the open Web. I do not suggest that we compromise our standards, but that we spend significant resources in making our resources and methods easily available to the world. How better for research libraries to advance the public good?

---

4 For an extended version of this argument, see Courant, P. N. (forthcoming), "Scholarship: The Wave of the Future in the Digital Age," in Richard N. Katz, ed., *The Tower and the Cloud: The Co-Evolution of Higher Education and the Web* (in press).

Co-Teaching: The Library and Me

Stephen G. Nichols

I've taught for more years than I care to think about. And throughout my career as a wandering scholar in the United States and Europe, libraries have always played an important, if stationary role: I wandered; they stayed put. At least they did until recently. In the past decade, more and more of my research needs—journal articles, bibliographic materials, reference books, dictionaries, and primary and secondary works of all kinds—have become instantly conjurable on my computer screen. Even more revolutionary is that I no longer have to remain in my office on campus to access these virtual stacks. Thanks to software such as VPN Secure Client, I call up the library's panoply of information from any place with Internet access. Needless to say, bringing the library with me on my travels has made preparing lectures and checking references a lot easier . . . to say nothing of lightening my luggage!

Exciting as it may be, the revolution in research resources is not exactly breaking news. The frontier today—and for the foreseeable future, I believe—lies in the challenge of what I like to call "co-teaching" with the library, namely, bringing the library into the classroom. That may seem like a logical extension of taking the library with you, but many colleagues who routinely use virtual resources for research tell me they have yet to explore these new pedagogical frontiers. Few dispute the rationale for combining teaching and research, but that frequently means using some part of the knowledge acquired from research to prepare classes. But doesn't that imply that teaching plays no active role in refining scholarly inquiry?

Such assumptions arise for a variety of reasons. One is that teaching and research involve distinctive modes of communication. Obviously, we convey ideas differently when we teach our students than when we lecture to our colleagues. With students, we are not simply demonstrating new ways of looking at a given problem. We

Stephen G. Nichols is James M. Beall Professor of French and Humanities at The Johns Hopkins University.

are also—even more crucially—explaining the context and history of the issue at hand. We are showing why this topic matters. This doesn't imply that we are less intently focused on our particular area of inquiry when we teach it. It does mean, however, seeing it through the eyes of those unfamiliar with our concerns.

Thinking about my teaching, I've realized how critical it is to reach students by exciting their interest. First, I must grasp what it is they find so strange—even alienating—about technically complex subjects. Secondly, I must determine a way to capture their attention. I've found that this means demonstrating what excites me about my work, for if I can't communicate my own enthusiasm, I can't expect others to share it. I must therefore let students see the drama of my research—the disappointments as well as the successes.

I've found that too often, we professors feel responsible for getting across facts, while leaving out the messy details of how we came by them. But teaching can add invaluably to our research when we are forced to remix highlights of our discoveries with the painstaking, even tedious efforts that produced them. This exercise comes with an important collateral benefit. Suddenly, as we share our work with students, the relevance and disciplinary logic of our research agenda comes into full focus as we encounter facets of the project we might never have seen. That's why it makes sense to develop pedagogical techniques focusing on the larger context of our research. And this is precisely where the library can enter the classroom with us to become a co-teacher.

Let me offer a "before and after" scenario of how this works. When I began teaching medieval French literature, I did it much the same way as my own professors had. That meant using a modern printed edition of the romances, epics, chronicles, dramas, or lyric poems chosen for the course. The editions used for graduate students offered the text in a version of the medieval French language, while undergraduate courses more often used 20th-century French translations, with a few samples of the original language to offer a medieval flavor. Since they were all modern editions or translations, the books appeared to students' eyes physically like those by modern authors.

When they opened these books prepared to read them as they would a modern work, they experienced a shock. Nothing had prepared them for a world so different from their own. The atmosphere, the sentiments, the exploits, the people described could not have seemed more alien to them. Knights dressed head-to-toe in armor breaking lances with opponents who erupted from the forest to challenge them with no apparent reason; noblewomen carried off from castles in full view of King Arthur and his knights; princes who turned into birds of prey; lords who left their beds at night to become werewolves; heroes who opposed untold numbers of enemy almost single-handedly. And what was all this business about courtly love?

Who could blame students for being confused? They were reading works wrenched from their historical setting, where the story would have appeared perfectly natural. It was my job to explain that historical background: language, customs, codes of chivalry, politics—in short, everything that made these works so different. But try as I might, the gulf remained. Many students found the medieval world remote and abstract. I could explain to them that these works were originally written by hand in richly decorated and illustrated manuscripts. But unless they could see the manuscripts themselves, how could they visualize what I was saying? How could they appreciate the columns of calligraphy, or wonder at the exquisitely painted miniatures depicting key scenes of knights and ladies dancing, castles, tournaments, battles, dragons, whimsical designs, and other signs of this lost art from a bygone era? If I could have shown these things to them, they would have learned much more because they would have been able to visualize the historical setting.

It's not that I did not manage to get some of these ideas across to the students, or that many of them did not enjoy the reading. My own enthusiasm proved infectious to some, but I don't flatter myself that I could ever do justice to the works as a whole. How could I have done so without being able to show them what the original work looked like? And how could I have done that? Manuscripts of the works I taught were housed in widely scattered libraries. In the era of the passive library, I would have had to take my class to cities all over Europe and North America. The libraries were not going to come to us! At least not in those days.

But what if the library could come to my classroom? Suppose it were possible to teach medieval literature from digital surrogates of the manuscripts so that students would be able to see the medieval work? I'm talking not about a passive image, but about a version of the original they could open and read on their computer screen. They would be able not only to read the stories in the original setting but also to see how books were produced by scribes and artists working together. For nonspecialists who could not be expected to decipher medieval scripts or read the old language, the digital surrogate would be an even more effective teaching tool. For, unlike a manuscript, the digital version would have transcriptions and notes to facilitate reading, translating, and studying the written text and images. That sounds reasonable, but what would it take to accomplish? And if we did manage to put manuscripts online, how would they change our teaching?

To answer the first question in detail would require an article in itself. Suffice it to say that for me to have fully functional manuscript surrogates in my classroom requires a research library willing to act as a digital repository. That library must dedicate staff and resources to collecting raw digital files of materials from widely dispersed institutional owners that agree to have the documents scanned and made available by the library. Once the mass of images has been acquired—no mean feat in itself—they must be organized and programmed according to a logical plan called an "intellectual data model" prepared by the library's digital curators. It is the data model that guides the programmers in adding the levels of functionality that allow digitized artifacts to appear on a computer screen.

Functional commands are the equivalent of hands that turn the pages of a manuscript: they replace the magnifying glass or ultraviolet light in revealing small details of the original; they allow us to obtain three-dimensional renditions of objects; they enable us to search for words or images, or to call up anything else we might need to look at. They can also assist in making comparisons and in many other tasks required for teaching or scholarship.

But where does the information in the data model come from? After all, the digital curators are not themselves going to teach these manuscripts or use them for research. That's our responsibility as scholars, of course. It is also why this new world of digitized archival resources binds our teaching and research so tightly, while linking both to the library. No matter how talented they are, digital curators can do their work effectively only after my colleagues and I tell them what we need. Ordinarily, this would not pose a problem since we usually work on or teach material we know. In this instance, circumstances were different. We were being asked to say how we wanted to work with and teach digitized manuscripts. What kinds of functions should the programmers design to meet our needs? The questions could not have been more straightforward, or more challenging. For it meant having to decide how to work and teach in an entirely new way.

It wasn't the material that was new—my colleagues and I had worked with the artifacts themselves, and taught them. It wasn't even the medium itself—we were familiar enough with the Internet. The novelty was the library's role: it was asking us to design teaching and research needs in advance. It was also offering a novel kind of access to our artifacts. Rather than having to study them one at a time in different places, we could now bring the artifacts into our studies and classrooms for research and teaching. We would be able to do things previously impossible, such as making side-by-side comparisons of manuscripts physically remote from one another. It would also be possible to show variant treatments of a work in manuscripts produced at different times.

Rather than having to teach a work as something fixed once and for all by its author, I could illustrate medieval book production as a participatory process in which scribes could alter passages to suit their own or their patrons' tastes. With numbers of manuscripts of the same work to consult, students could study the dramatic changes in the style and content of illustrations over time. These simple historical facts could simply not be effectively conveyed when teaching from the fixed text of a printed edition.

But unprecedented access to our material would have other implications. For example, having more than 150 manuscripts of a single work produced over a period of 200 years, we realized, would also generate data on a scale we'd never dreamed of. For each manuscript was unique, differing in subtle and not-so-subtle ways from the others. Collectively, they constitute nothing short of a new perspective on medieval literature. In consequence, our focus would have to expand beyond the internal dynamics of plot, language, and structure to consider the rich variety of manuscript presentation evolved over centuries. We would need to propose new questions and research problems, and respond to new teaching challenges. The library could deliver access to make this possible, but first we had to rethink what we were asking them for. This is a challenge with which we are still grappling, as more and more codices come on line. But that's another story.

Once I began teaching from manuscript surrogates, I found that the library had online resources to make classes even more productive. Here's a description of what has become a typical class using these new resources. We're studying a 13th-century romance. I begin by projecting a page or folio on the screen in front of the class. I ask students to take turns deciphering and translating lines, while I comment on the grammatical points of medieval French. Suddenly, they come to a word they don't recognize. Thanks to the library's subscription to an online Old French dictionary, I open another browser tab, call up the dictionary, and try to look up the word as it appears in the manuscript. Students are puzzled at not finding it. That isn't surprising, I tell them. Orthographic conventions didn't exist in the Middle Ages. People tended to spell words phonetically, but because people in each region spoke with a different accent, the same word could be pronounced, and thus spelled, in a variety of ways. I reel off some variations for the word we're looking for. Thus prompted, the students easily locate the word in the online dictionary.

They see that the entry for the word in question gives a number of variants, as well as references to the word as it appears in other medieval texts. After brief discussion, a student asks if the meanings of words varied as much as their spelling (particularly in comparison with modern French). Whereas once I would simply have answered the question, now we have resources that let the students work out the answer. Opening yet another browser window, we call up one of the other medieval works cited in the dictionary entry from a database to which the library also subscribes. In an instant, we have the passage. The students read it, proposing possible meanings for the word that might fit the context. They discover that the meaning that fits the passage we're reading in class is indeed somewhat different from the one they find in the new citation.

This leads another student to ask whether the variations in meaning could be affected by the differing syntax in each passage. Good question, and one that we can also research online as a class. While the answers are less definitive than in the case of spelling or meaning, the exercise introduces the students to yet another resource available through the library. At the same time, I get the opportunity to explain examples of Old French syntax in a context they are more likely to profit from because the discussion has stemmed from their own question.

As the class proceeds, the students unselfconsciously adopt a number of different professional roles: literary critic, philologist, lexicographer, historical linguist, and grammarian. They've become archeologists, seeking to make sense of an historical enigma made up of archaic language, pictures of a vanished world, strange social codes, and unfamiliar expressions. More important, they have done so as a class working together, fueled by collective curiosity. Class dynamics do not lack for a healthy tension spurred by amicable competition as students vie to find solutions to each other's questions. Would their excitement be so palpable if they were not face-to-face with the historical object? Judging from student reactions to the same material that I used to teach from printed editions, the answer is a resounding no.

Since we live in an age of outcomes assessment, it's fair to ask whether students actually learn more in this new environment. How could it be otherwise? After all, they have a much more varied—and above all interactive—experience with the material than do students who simply read a medieval work in a modern critical edition. Seeing the work in a variety of settings affords students an opportunity to understand not just the work but also the changing public of the period. They learn to distinguish between a 13th-century codex, as opposed to one produced 200 years later—and to pride themselves on their discernment.

The library extends their competence by enlisting them as assistants for the digital library. Students perform key aspects of the "back-end" work that enables functionality for the surrogates. For example, they are needed for the tagging that allows viewers to search manuscripts, to navigate through them, and to perform other functions. Such work can be done only by someone who can read the original. The same is true for transcriptions of manuscripts. Students have progressively played key roles in transcribing works as they have gone online. In some instances, transcription projects have been undertaken as a semester-long class assignment. At other times, students have volunteered. In all cases, however, the combination of classroom and extracurricular involvement with the library's digital library means that students today have greater familiarity with manuscripts and the works they represent than their predecessors ever did.

In closing, let me hasten to put my own experience in context. What is unusual at Johns Hopkins is not the digitization of manuscripts. There are a good many such projects. Rather it is the fact that from the outset, the Johns Hopkins Digital Manuscript Library was conceived as a library initiative that involved scholars. That is the reverse of the usual scenario, where scholars undertake digitization projects on their own, enlisting the assistance of the library as needed. Indeed, one finds digital humanities centers whose Web sites make little or no mention of the libraries that support research at their universities—and, one imagines, a good deal of the inquiry that takes place in the digital centers themselves. It would be gratuitous to cite particular examples, even if randomly chosen from my recent reading on the subject. While it may simply be an oversight that the Web sites of digital humanities projects do not acknowledge the role of their research library, I think the problem runs deeper. Faculty members in the humanities tend to see themselves as belonging to the School of Arts and Sciences. Since the library is often a separate division in the organization of the typical research university, faculty do not think to credit the library's role in their enterprise.

But time and resources are on the side of the library. More than ever, research libraries generate projects once seen as the province of scholars working alone. Individual faculty now perceive that research libraries have become the venue for large-scale digital enterprises. If they wish to advance their projects, faculty will have to work with their library colleagues—not only a gain for the undertaking itself but also a sure winner when they go to teach it. At least that's what I have found.

The Role of the Library in 21st-Century Scholarly Publishing

Kate Wittenberg

Introduction

As research and scholarship move increasingly into the digital arena, the processes and organizations involved in the publication of this work must evolve as well. The changing landscape of libraries, publishers, and scholarly societies; university views on tenure and digital scholarship; the emerging role of search engines; and the continuing development of information technology have created a need for radical rethinking of the roles of the major players in scholarly communication. We need to understand how users create, discover, and evaluate information, as well as the real and virtual environments in which they do their academic work, in order to plan our scholarly communication and e-publishing strategies for the future. In the past, discussions of change in scholarly communication have often focused on the use of new technologies. Going forward, the conversation needs to focus on the less technical, but perhaps even more complex, issues of changing user needs, different organizational structures, new kinds of jobs, and partnerships among the key organizations involved in knowledge dissemination.

One of the key players in the changing information landscape is the research library and its professional staff. With their deep understanding of how to organize, store, and deliver information, the tools and functionality that add value to digital content, and the changing habits of users, librarians have the potential to play a leading role in moving forward with new models of scholarly communication. With the additional benefit of a robust and stable information technology infrastructure, the research library is in a position to provide both the platform and many of the skills needed to enable the creation of new forms of scholarship and to disseminate the resulting content to a wide audience of users. Whether the library can or should take on this role depends upon a number of factors, but the primary issue

Kate Wittenberg is a consultant in scholarly communication and electronic publishing. From 1999 to 2008 she was Director of the Electronic Publishing Initiative at Columbia University.

is how its leaders see the library's role in the new information landscape, and whether they can establish effective partnerships with publishers, faculty, and information technology organizations within their institutions. The challenges that lie ahead are too complex to be solved by one player. They can be addressed effectively only through collaboration, and the creation of new kinds of hybrid organizations and staff. Whether research libraries will be part of these new organizations depends on the role that they carve out for themselves in the rapidly evolving environment.

New Publishing Models for New Readers

Scholars and students have become technically skilled consumers of digital information, and they have high expectations regarding its format, functionality, and delivery. This makes it essential that we redefine the appropriate role for publishers in this information environment. We must begin to understand the strategies that scholars are using in creating their work and the most useful roles for information professionals such as librarians, information technology staff, and publishers. First, we will need to incorporate a new perspective into the traditional publishing process by acknowledging scholars as active collaborators in the creation of new kinds of resources within their disciplines. As publishers, we must begin to view ourselves as researchers who play a role in leading innovation in a discipline through the creation of new models of scholarship, tools, and dissemination, but we will do this as collaborators with our authors. We will bring to the table an understanding of the scholarly process, peer review, editorial development, technical capacity, and users' needs. As our authors come with a vision of the possibilities presented in a multimedia publishing environment, publishers will have to develop an equally innovative vision of their role in this collaborative process.

Authors and their publishers will share in considering questions such as the following: Must scholarly narrative necessarily be presented in linear form? Are there new ways to present an "authorial voice" while allowing readers to structure the way in which they encounter a work? Are images and data supplementary evidence for points made in the text, or can they now become central organizing structures of a work? Is there value in being able to search thematically across many different works of scholarship in order to connect information in new ways? What new kinds of resources can be created by integrating research and teaching materials? And can digital publications actually become a place where collaboration occurs, thus creating yet another form of publication in the process? All of these questions, which are still theoretical in most fields of scholarship, become critical once the answers can actually be implemented in a digital publication. But what are the skills and attitudes that publishing professionals must possess in order to help authors sort through the questions and come up with useful and practical answers?

First, editors (who are normally on the front lines in terms of encountering authors during the research, planning, and writing process) must start to see themselves as researchers who work with authors in creating new models of scholarship rather than as staff who react to scholarly work once it is submitted in completed form for publication. Second, editors must begin to think more creatively about the organization and presentation of information in terms of how readers encounter their publications. Editors will need to educate themselves in the use of digital resources and how this use changes the way in which we present scholarly content and tools. The publication process must become a shared endeavor in which authors, librarians, information technologists, and readers form a team that relies on the skills, experience, perspectives, and habits brought to the table by each of its members. This is an area in which there exists a tremendous potential for librarians, with their expertise in information architecture, cataloging and indexing, and content management, and their understanding of the changing habits of users in their search for information.

Will librarians become editors? Will editors become librarians? Or will a new type of job emerge that requires expertise in both of these fields? The new model for publishing requires someone who understands the intellectual environment in various disciplines, identifies the scholars working most productively in those fields, and works with those scholars to enable the successful completion and publication of a scholarly work. It also requires someone who understands the role of metadata, search and discovery, and preservation and access. A position that brings together these two kinds of experience would open exciting possibilities for creating new models of publishing appropriate for the current environment.

A Focus on Users

New publishing models have emerged from a variety of sources, including research libraries, government-funded projects, professional societies, and commercial publishing. One element that is common to several of these models is a strong focus on users—their emerging needs and preferences in doing their work—and less concern than in the past with publishing within traditional categories such as journals, books, databases, and reference works. These new initiatives demonstrate an interest in providing resources, information, tools, and services that fulfill the needs of the user; whether or not the resulting resources look like traditional publications is of secondary concern. What is important is that the product satisfies a user's need to access important content in his or her field, and that includes the tools and functionality that make the content timely and useful. In this new publishing model, the greatest measure of value becomes the content's utility and functionality for a defined set of users, rather than any "objective" measure of quality.

In creating these kinds of publications, libraries have an advantage over traditional publishers in that they have fewer preconceived notions about what the market requires. Rather than attempting to re-create traditional print publications in digital form, they can focus on disseminating information and services that respond to users' needs in whatever form seems most appropriate to the content. Because librarians can think like users as a result of their experience in responding to scholars and students, they will be in a strong position to chart the way for new models for shaping and delivering scholarly information.

Information Literacy

An important issue to consider in new publishing models is the complex relationship between the "closed" world of the researcher's traditional work environment and the "open" world of the Web. The vast amount of information now available can be either a benefit or an obstacle to effective research, writing, and teaching, depending on how successfully users manage this information and how they are able to make it relevant to their own work. While some scholars clearly demonstrate a desire to explore freely and contribute as participants to the vast array of content and tools available through the Web, it is becoming equally clear that in many cases they would like some level of selectivity and guidance concerning how to identify and then evaluate the information they find. They also need assurance that they will receive academic credit for the work that they disseminate through this environment. In their Web-based social environments, scholars and students are using sophisticated mechanisms for sharing information in collaborative spaces. Increasingly, they are using these networked spaces as a means for communicating with colleagues, and some publishers are already creating collaborative spaces to accompany their content. An important issue to consider going forward is how to make such environments useful for scholarly research and dissemination.

These discussions raise the larger issue of information literacy in the emerging digital environment. How will publishers help users separate high-quality, peer-reviewed content from other information that is easily available through search mechanisms? How do publishers "brand" their material in the digital environment? And are users actually creating new ways of evaluating content that are different from those with which publishers are comfortable? For example, in many social networked environments the community itself decides whether to allow a new participant the status that permits certain levels of access and its associated privileges (e.g., the ability to read and exchange profiles and messages, participate in conversations, edit previously posted content). Many users have become comfortable with this method of evaluating content credibility, which imitates, in many ways, the trusted-peer models used in evaluating social interactions, such as asking a friend what new musical groups are good or where to go on vacation. The question of whether this community-based evaluation model will translate to the assessment of scholarly and educational content, however, has yet to be answered.

This system for establishing credibility in a social networked environment is in sharp contrast to the top-down peer review system used for years by the academic world. The traditional system leaves the end user out of the quality assessment process, as it is handled before content ever appears in final, published form. In this system, the authority to establish credibility rests with the publisher rather than with the community of users, and increasingly may be in opposition to the community-based model. As scholars continue to use and develop networked environments, the status of having one's work approved by a community's members may exceed the credibility gained through traditional peer review. As this process evolves, we may see a broader transformation in which research and scholarly publishing become a process of participation in a community rather than of receiving the imprimatur of an "expert." In this case, publishers will have to confront the issue of how to allow peer networking, participation, and interaction to take on increasing value without lowering quality standards or disseminating erroneous information through a scholarly or educational publication. Here again, librarians, who have historically connected scholars and students to appropriate content, may emerge as key players in the process of evaluating content.

The Role of Information Professionals

It is clear that mechanisms for creating, finding, and evaluating scholarly content are undergoing rapid development and change in the current digital environment and that new models for academic publishing are needed. It is still unclear, however, who will create the new models. Will the traditional arbiters of content quality, such as libraries and scholarly publishers, step up together to propose new models? Or will scholars establish and implement systems for assessing credibility and disseminating their work on their own? If the library and publishing communities can move quickly to incorporate users' interests in new forms of scholarship, collaboration and community-based networks, and multimedia technologies in designing new scholarly resources, they will be in a much stronger position.

Developing these kinds of publications, however, will require a change in mindset within the established library and publishing communities. Professionals in these fields will need to initiate conversations with each other, as well as with new players and partners. Developers of Web-based social communities, commercial search engines, manufacturers of electronic devices, and scholars themselves will necessarily become advisors and collaborators. Market research (for publishers) and outreach (for libraries) will include arranging focused discussions with scholars and students, participating in ongoing academic conversations concerning publication and criteria for tenure and promotion, and engaging deeply at many levels with the scholarly research community.

The Need for Experimentation

It will be important for publishers and librarians together to engage in experiments that test various models for creating and disseminating content. They might, for example, develop Web-based resources that allow easy transitions between a scholar's research at an early stage of development, a reference to the same scholar's body of published work through a more formal library, and a further reference to a collaborative community in which colleagues in related fields offer their perspectives on the work being presented. In such an environment, users might have a choice of reading the early-stage writing or research data, searching or browsing additional related resources in a larger digital library, asking for guidance from a librarian who is a member of the virtual collaborative community, or communicating directly with the author regarding his or her research findings. As scholars have the ability to examine the provenance, authenticity, and the multiple contexts from which items in their research environment arise, observant and innovative publishers will be able to understand how to provide and structure content in ways that are appropriate to the evolving needs of users.

Such experiments might also shed light on the relative value that users attach to the evaluation of information by peers, librarians, and publishers. In addition to discussions concerning appropriate technology and design, this conversation needs to include a focus on less technical, but perhaps more intractable, issues: changing assumptions about quality and credibility of content, reconsidering attitudes toward peer review and academic advancement, and acknowledging authors and readers as active collaborators in the creation of new kinds of scholarly resources and publications.

Sustainability

Another area requiring attention and leadership is the development of innovative and effective business models for sustaining digital resources. Business planning plays a critical role in this environment and provides one of the most interesting areas for experimentation. Business planning in this field requires having a grasp of real costs. Models for covering those costs include subscription-based revenue streams, open access funded by university budgets, or grant funding for individual projects or collective infrastructure/staffing. All these projects come with significant costs, whether we call the resulting resources open access or revenue-supported projects.

Going forward, we will need new business models that support the innovative and collaborative e-publishing partnerships that are starting to form. In developing these models, we need to make a clear distinction between cost-recovery mechanisms for not-for-profit publishing and the pricing practices of the large commercial publishers (that is, the discussion needs to be more than a simple debate over "open access" versus "price gouging"). Someone has to pay for all this work. Whether we call it publishing, institutional repositories, or scholarly communication, there must be a source of funds to develop and maintain these projects and the professional staff who make them work. If we ignore this fact, we will never move ahead in this discussion. To make progress in this area, we need to engage in an honest and reality-based level of discourse that acknowledges the needs of both libraries and publishers and that moves beyond divisive rhetoric.

Conclusion

For many years, publishers have operated as self-sufficient businesses, with the publishing processes taking place within the confines of the organization, and being done by people with traditional publishing experience. Now we need to bring in new skill sets not only for the design, production, and dissemination of scholarly products but also for the management of collaborations and partnerships and for the operation of a complex organizational structure. The keys to moving forward effectively include an ability to understand our users and their changing behavior, a willingness to experiment, and an appreciation of hybrid organizations that take advantage of skills contributed by players with diverse backgrounds and experience. Leadership of such a team will require an understanding of the various players and the value of their contributions, as well as a clear and imaginative view of the future information landscape. It will at times be difficult to accept the changes that collaborations bring and to manage them productively, but ignoring the challenge will mean the possible loss of an opportunity for both publishers and librarians to make an important contribution to the landscape that is being created.

A New Value Equation Challenge: The Emergence of eResearch and Roles for Research Libraries

Richard E. (Rick) Luce

Emergence of eScience

A convergence of exponential increases in computing, storage, online sensors, and bandwidth enabling collaboration in new ways has led to the rise of eScience. Characterized by large-scale, distributed global collaboration using distributed information technologies, eScience is supported by the next generation of cyberinfrastructure. eScience is typically conducted by a multidisciplinary team working on problems that have only become solvable in recent years with improved data collection and data analysis capabilities.

These characteristics fundamentally alter the ways in which scientists carry out their work, the tools and workflows they use, the types of problems they address, and the communications resulting from their research. The revolutionary potential of eScience is the ability to work at a much greater scale and intensity using distributed networks and powerful tools. Examples range from distributed computational astronomy to complex systems such as social networks, climate changes, multifactorial diseases, and pollution remediation.

Virtually every field in science and engineering has been changed by the convergence of these technologies, yielding entirely new ways of thinking about and understanding physical, biological, and social phenomena.[1] These revolutionary developments will require a corresponding disruptive change in the ways in which libraries serve scientists' needs.

Rick Luce is Vice Provost and Director of Libraries at Emory University.

1 The 2020 Science Group. 2002. Towards 2020 Science. Redmond, Wash.: Microsoft Corporation. Available at http://research.microsoft.com/towards2020science/background_overview.htm.

A Growing Convergence: eResearch

While these new eScience developments initially characterized only the science, technology, engineering, and medicine disciplines, that distinction has faded; we now see these developments beginning to penetrate the social sciences and the humanities. The rise of transdisciplinary work, coupled with social scholarship—which is characterized by openness and the use of social tools, including virtual conversations, access, sharing, collaboration, and transparent revision—will continue to erode boundaries.

Corresponding with increased engagement in the social sciences and humanities is the broader notion of eResearch. eResearch refers to the development of, and the support for, advanced information and computational technologies to enhance all phases of research processes. A fundamental enabler of innovations and new discoveries, eResearch is becoming just as critical for the advancement of the social sciences and the humanities as it already is in the sciences.

Implications for Research Libraries

Preserving knowledge is one of the most vital and rapidly changing fundamental roles of the research library. For libraries that are now positioning themselves to support eResearch, preserving knowledge entails at least four key challenges:

- ensuring the quality, integrity, and curation of digital research information;
- sustaining today's evolving digital service environments;
- bridging and connecting different worlds, disciplines, and paradigms for knowing and understanding; and
- archiving research data in a data world.

Discussion surrounding support of eResearch environments has focused on the overwhelming volume of data produced, with attendant challenges of scaling up capture and preservation capabilities. The more significant challenge, however, is the changing paradigm for capturing and reflecting research communication in an eResearch environment. Instead of simply storing objects of assorted types, researchers need libraries that reflect a Web 2.0 service environment in which communication is continuous and synchronous. This reality introduces significantly greater complexity to digital capture, curation, and preservation.

Innovative thinking is essential; a few existing lessons from external models tackling grand challenge problems are instructive. Institutional organizational silos alone cannot scale sufficiently to support this environment; the challenge requires transnational approaches and a matrix of capabilities. The speed of organizational deployment matters. The ability to move quickly and with agility is a competitive asset; slow-moving organizations are severely handicapped in this environment. Continuous adaptation is required; a diversity of approaches resulting in a variety of experiments should be celebrated.

Supporting Creation: A Key Role

A shift is emerging in the importance of different products of research. Increasingly, value is placed not on the publication(s) resulting from a research project but on the data-modeling and data-generation phases that occur earlier in the research life cycle. This shift to a more dynamic and collaborative process of doing science has led to a less formal means of communicating. In some areas of science this is leading to a less well-defined medium that is part publication and part ongoing communication process. Supporting this shift requires actively enabling and sustaining these communication processes rather than simply archiving the end result as a formal publication. Librarians and informaticians must be involved in the early planning and data-modeling phases of eResearch to ensure the collection, preservation, ease of use, and availability of data today and in the future.

There is a need for workflow tools that capture emerging communication modalities, and libraries and appropriate partners have the opportunity to fill that critical gap. It is at this early creation stage that the establishment of policies concerning data description, management, access, and sharing should be addressed, with particular attention paid to the demand for unfettered access to the research literature corpora. The level of knowledge and engagement required to effectively fill this role, however, goes well beyond knowledge of the literature. It requires being a trusted member of the community with recognized authority in information-related matters. This new paradigm entails shifting library foci from managing specialized collections to emphasizing proactive outreach and engagement.

Connecting Communities: A Second Key Role

The interactions required to facilitate eResearch differ in time and space from other methods. As a neutral commons, research libraries could provide collaborative facilities that allow startup efforts to congeal and connections to evolve. Centering startup activities within these co-laboratory facilities provides rich opportunities to connect with, and consult on, data practices ranging from collection and description to publication and preservation. Success, however, will require far more dynamic and proactive engagement than current institutional repository models do.

In the virtual world a neutral mechanism to create community interactions is needed. Groups conducting research will need access to information in collaborative Web spaces. These collaborative Web spaces will be populated by information feeds customized for individual teams of researchers. Some of these feeds will be customized for researchers fitting specific profiles; others will be pulled from external sites. Still others will be created by intelligent agents crawling the Web, remote repositories, and local resources.

Hybrid teams of information science experts working closely with researchers would determine the information requirements for these Web spaces. After determining the requirements, staff members would create and customize information feeds, serving as RSS channel editors and using tools to aggregate and filter RSS feeds from external sites. They could augment artificial intelligence with human intelligence by creating search strategies for intelligent agents with the help of taxonomies that map current terms to emerging terms, and terms from one domain to another domain.

Support for social networks through advanced social software capabilities is another potential service for research libraries. Social software in an eResearch environment has three dimensions: (1) conversational interactions, in which software applications facilitate synchronous and asynchronous communication among individuals and groups; (2) collaborative social networks, which allow individuals to discover and interact with colleagues who have related interests; and (3) social feedback systems, which use behavioral data, such as statistical log analyses, to create relationships and evaluative metrics.

One additional dimension of connection via the commons bears mentioning. Libraries can be the conveners that establish a common ground among different players. Collaboration and partnering are essential in the eResearch environment. While some organizations will specialize in building tools and others in building relationships, both are required.

Curation: A Third Key Role

The generation of vast amounts of primary data gives rise to data-curation questions. Data used to be hidden behind office walls, scribbled in notebooks, stored in file cabinets, and recorded on hard drives. Now data are more often "loose" and available to be repurposed and recombined. Caring for these data requires life cycle data management, covering acquisition and integration, treatment, provenance, persistence, and digital preservation.

Over the next five years we will collect more scientific data than we have collected in all of human history. Access and cross-domain usage of distributed collections is highly dependent upon the application of uniform methods of description when the data are created. Metadata are an essential component of research data. Research libraries can lead the development of standardized, ontologically rich automated metadata for such data sets. Developing and managing metadata are already established tasks in the library community—although current practices will not handle the scale envisioned. The pervasive use of machine-aided semantic annotation, using well-structured metadata, is the only feasible approach for effectively organizing and describing eResearch data.

Standardizing approaches to metadata collection is fundamental, and metadata must be a required part of the eResearch communication process. We should not underestimate the cost and effort that will be required to collect metadata on this scale—nor can we underestimate the cost to redo it if not done properly. Given the challenges of scale, the potential of socially tagging data—similar to the process of social bookmarking currently used to catalog photos on Flickr—should be robustly explored.

With the rise of the semantic Web, we can forecast the age of distributed personal publication, a new paradigm where individuals and teams publish their own results, rather than relying on conventional centralized databases with their corresponding curatorial staff. Future eResearch will include communication about a variety of dimensions surrounding data, published locally by individuals, institutional or domain repositories, or the next generation of journals, complete with semantically rich metadata.

Research libraries could take responsibility for assisting with curation and preservation of smaller-scale data repositories arising from the work of local or domain-specific research groups. The level of description used with research data is critical to discovering new ways of combining and using data. Research libraries focusing on their core competencies are well positioned to lead this strategic work.

Developing the Supporting Infrastructure

Research libraries will be best served by focusing on their critical core competencies while partnering with other organizational players. It is already clear that public and nonprofit institutions, no matter how large, will be singularly unable to meet the ever-expanding massive-scale data storage needs of eScience projects, such as the Large Synoptic Survey Telescope project, which generates 30 terabytes of data nightly. Whether aggregations of public or academic research communities banding together will be up to the task remains unclear.

Compounding the issue of scale are the challenges of providing adequate electrical power to run the necessary storage and server farms. Today, electrical power and cost per megawatt are the limiting factors in expanding large data centers. This is driving the global corporate push toward distributed computing infrastructures. Regardless of the many far-reaching public policy issues inherent in privatizing research data, economies of scale have positioned the private sector as a serious player for cyberinfrastructure support in the United States.

Because digital component performance is continually improving, the scale of information technology (IT) environments is constantly increasing. As a result, IT networks are best managed as a unified "whole." This "cloud computing," also known as "fabric," "application virtualization," and "datacenter virtualization," involves linking large pools of systems to provide IT services. This approach allows corporate data centers to operate more like the Internet by enabling computing across a distributed, globally accessible fabric of resources, rather than only on local machines or remote server farms. The private sector, with more investment capital and experience running massive data farms, is aggressively positioning itself for this role. Yahoo, Google, IBM, and Microsoft have announced initiatives to promote new software development methods that will help researchers address the challenges of Internet-scale eScience applications in the future.

Morphing Digital Research Libraries

The coming eResearch tsunami will profoundly affect the role of research libraries today and tomorrow. The scale of change confronting research libraries is unprecedented, and successfully responding will require disruptive thinking and novel solutions.

The dominance of Google's search services, book digitization program, organization of information in the broader context, and ubiquitous presence constantly challenge research libraries to more finely focus their role in information delivery. In addition, researchers create and use massive data sets, and increasingly rely on inter-disciplinary teams—not subject-specific colleagues—from numerous institutions around the globe. The grand challenge for research libraries will be to provide data services to researchers in the new era.

A variety of integrated, end-user information resources, all of which ideally should be available in accessible user environments, are missing today. A cursory list includes profiles of scientists and research groups; toolkits for data integration, text and data mining analysis, and validation; registries of instruments and sensors; registries of software toolkits; registries of data sets; and more.

Professionals responsible for managing such data repository collections are beginning to be called data scientists. They could just as well be data librarians or informationists. Regardless of the label, this is an emerging profession; libraries could play a significant role in building teams of professionals ready to assume these roles. Further, eResearch data collections tend to be distributed, requiring coordination across institutions. Research libraries have a long tradition of creatively coordinating resource sharing across multiple institutions. Putting this concept on steroids, they could work in the same vein with distributed data collections.

First on our priority list ought to be formulating new partnerships with data-driven researchers—in all fields. Libraries can foster collaboration networks and provide collaboration space (both virtual and physical) where researchers can work, in addition to building institutional data repositories.

New Organizational Structures

New hybrid organizations likely will emerge to tackle questions surrounding long-term custodianship of data repositories. It is premature to predict which organization(s) will succeed at that task. Any number of organizations, including commercial ventures, the grid community, supercomputer centers, research libraries, dedicated research groups, or new organizations we have not yet envisioned, could combine capabilities to ensure success.

Research libraries have traditionally been structured and staffed around disciplines. In contrast, eResearch embraces multidisciplinary approaches. eScience often requires virtual teams to form dynamically in the initial planning phases of a research project, work on a project, and then morph into something else when a less intense presence is needed. This requires fluid staffing structures and a more dynamic structural model than our current practice of assigning departmental or subject liaisons. Such professionals may be well integrated, but are not usually able to dynamically respond to emerging trends with intense needs. The agility required to mobilize support in this environment will require research libraries to work seamlessly across institutional boundaries.

New organizational models should reflect the environments they are attempting to support, recognizing the synergy and interdependence between scholars and information pioneers. To proactively support this environment, librarians must become part of the research process—full members of the research team. To do this, library staff members need to "go native" and embed themselves among the teams they support. Clearly this will have significant implications for the library's staffing profile and workforce skill set.

What Research Libraries Can Do Now

At this stage, research libraries should focus on developing the functional requirements of a data-archiving infrastructure, and let the appropriate organizational forms emerge from those requirements. As with any paradigm shift, there are many challenges and opportunities for organizations that have the agility to adapt and move quickly, as well as for new players.

Changes in research libraries must be driven by and reflect the needs of the research communities they seek to support. Researchers will expect the same level of ubiquitous convenience and advanced capabilities from their reconstructed digital libraries as they get from widely available eScience workflows. Our responses will require a shift in focus from delivering products (e.g., reference services or publications) to process (e.g., supporting team science).

Collaboration, partnerships, and de facto best practices are vital for researchers to exploit heterogeneous sources of data. Many types of organizations including research centers, libraries, supercomputing centers, archives, and Internet companies have expertise in some dimension of data-driven scholarship. Such expertise is nearly always incidental to the major expertise of the organization. The challenges facing research libraries are to articulate and advance our role and unique capabilities into the virtual laboratory environment. Success will require developing a deep anticipatory understanding of what these researchers require to perform their work successfully.

Limited space precludes more than the briefest sketch of other transformation opportunities, among which are the following:
- a transparent system of grid-like libraries and library data services supporting data science and curation;

- formation of eResearch communities that are multidisciplinary and international;
- support for personal information management, as data sets and associated information become increasingly portable; and
- a research agenda and development of sustained information science research capabilities.

Economic Sustainability: A Grand Challenge

Adequate and sustained funding for long-lived data collections and their associated facilities remains a vexing problem, spawning a call for creative approaches both nationally and internationally. Data preservation facilities must be able to support and provide for their collections over the long term. However, the widely decentralized and nonstandard mechanisms for generating data of every type and format imaginable make this problem an order of magnitude more difficult than our experiences to date with archiving and preservation. Infrastructure needs to be funded to enable research, and we need to be prepared to make the point repeatedly that libraries are part of the infrastructure.

Many questions remain to be resolved, such as:
- Who owns the data, especially when it is collaboratively collected?
- Who can access the data, and under what use and export conditions?
- Which research data need to be retained, for how long, and in what format(s)?
- What level of data reliability is required?
- Who pays the costs for curation and preservation, and for what period(s) of time?

In an era of information, software, and systems openness, we control less and less. The cost of owning and managing data, hardware, and software is very high. How do we offset and share multi-institutional infrastructure investments? Because it takes a community to meet these challenges, how many research libraries need to work together to meet specific eResearch needs, and how do we collaborate in new, more effective ways? There are many questions for which we do not have the answers. Research libraries ought to be committed to finding them.

Conclusion

The emergence of eResearch, with its associated large data repositories, heralds not only a new way of doing science but also a challenging new world for libraries, provided that we aggressively seize the opportunities. Traditional library roles—those of organization, access, and preservation—must be augmented by new capabilities in automatically describing, annotating, and manipulating a wide spectrum of collaborative, data-intensive information resources. Spanning the gamut of capabilities from raw data to informal and formal communications, the ability to discover and track research results remains an essential, although radically different-looking, component of the research infrastructure. A powerful user-centric infrastructure that supports collaborative multidisciplinary science is now required. A grand challenge now faces us: the next generation of research infrastructure requires dynamic data repositories. Are we ready to step up to center stage?

Related Sources

Berman, Francine, and Henry Brady. 2005. *Final Report: NSF SBE-CISE Workshop on Cyberinfrastructure and the Social Sciences.* Available at vis.sdsc.edu/sbe/reports/SBE-CISE-FINAL.pdf.

National Science Foundation. 2003. *Revolutionizing Science and Engineering through Cyberinfrastructure: Report of the National Science Foundation Blue Ribbon Advisory Panel on Cyberinfrastructure.* Available at http://www.nsf.gov/od/oci/reports/toc.jsp.

National Science Foundation Cyberinfrastructure Council. 2007. *Cyberinfrastructure Vision for 21st Century Discovery.* Available at http://www.nsf.gov/od/oci/CI_Vision_March07.pdf.

Welshons, Marlo, ed. 2006. *Our Cultural Commonwealth: The Report of the American Council of Learned Societies Commission on Cyberinfrastructure for the Humanities and Social Sciences.* New York, N.Y.: American Council of Learned Societies. Available at http://www.acls.org/programs/Default.aspx?id=644.

Accelerating Learning and Discovery: Refining the Role of Academic Librarians

Andrew Dillon

Introduction

There is a reasonable case to be made that academic libraries have changed more in the past two decades than in the preceding two centuries. Technology is a major driver, of that there is no dispute, as are the rising costs of publications and services. But the real questions of interest are less the nature of these technological innovations, spectacular as they may be, and more the social impacts and processes that have resulted. Furthermore, we must address these changes with the recognition that they have only begun, and that they are irreversible.

The 2002 National Academies report *Preparing for the Revolution* presented the challenge of universities operating in a completely digital environment, speculating on massive shifts in practices in the coming decades.[1] The Taiga Forum, a group of academic librarians, issued a set of provocative statements about academic libraries that suggested rapidly shrinking physical collections in the near term, an influx of young, MBA-like professionals to the workforce who would be unrecognizable as librarians, and the merger of academic computing with libraries on most campuses within five years. Couple these predictions to the latest National Endowment for the Arts report of further declines in literacy rates, and the shifts we face in both resources and users appear dramatic.[2]

The preponderance of digital resources now demanded by researchers and students is certainly altering library collections, and

Andrew Dillon is Dean of the School of Information at the University of Texas.

[1] *Preparing for the Revolution: Information Technology and the Future of the Research University*. 2002. Report of the National Research Council of the National Academies, National Academies Press. Available at http://www.arts.gov/research/ResearchReports_chrono.html.

[2] *To Read or Not to Read: A Question of National Consequence*. 2007. National Endowment for the Arts, Research Report #47, November 2007. http://www.arts.gov.

the data from our own school admissions office reveal that the average age of graduate students in our program has dropped below 30 and stayed there for the past few years. But what does this really mean for libraries? Collections do not disappear, and the paperless world seems less attainable now than it was a decade ago. Special collections become more valuable over time. It can be argued that libraries are a means, not an end, yet we seem to be suffering from a lack of understanding of our means. Worse, it appears that the profession of librarianship as taught and practiced in many environments is unclear how it can offer real value without retreating into the stock defenses of our role as the gatekeepers of quality, guarantors of access, and the sole possessors of the true knowledge of cataloging.

Library as System

While it has become popular in recent years to emphasize the library as place, an academic library is better viewed as a complex sociotechnical system that serves multiple stakeholders. Each stakeholder has expectations, needs, and understandings of the library, but not all stakeholders are direct users. Consequently, there is a tendency to place the end-user perspective at the forefront of discussions of the library's future. While it is important to be user-centric in design and implementation, to shape the form of successful future academic libraries we must address the broader context of all stakeholder needs. User-centered design in sociotechnical terms is not a popularity contest; it is a process of informed decision making intended to advance a solution that serves the demonstrable needs of an intended community. In this realm, what people say they like is not always what works best for them, and what people tell you they need at one point almost certainly shifts once you begin to deliver it. It is this dynamic interplay of need and solution in the evolution of new technologies that places academic libraries in such an ambiguous state.

The demands of university students for online anytime access will not lessen, and many libraries clearly view their physical environments as social spaces for laptop-carrying, coffee-drinking learners, invoking terms like "commons" and "learning rooms" to convey the shift of emphasis from collection to user. All well and good, as this is bringing people to the space where their walk-in can be counted as a positive statistic. It is less clear, however, what impact this bringing of bodies to a room actually has on the delivery of information to enquiring minds when their first point of enquiry remains the Google box. As libraries become more concerned with creating social spaces, they should also be concerned with entering into the people space, the library as accelerator, where information is sought, communicated, shared, tagged, and mined. Without taking this second step, the library adds little value over a bookstore.

Some might argue that the quality of access to digital collections is continually improving, so with more space for people and increased understanding of digital tools and collections, we are faced only with security and economic concerns while we proceed with business as usual. In this simple scenario, younger librarians will bring us the technology skills, shrinking collections will provide the new physical space, and those MBA-oriented professionals entering our field will help solve the management and financial problems. Once academic libraries merge with academic computing in a new, tuition-supported model of service provision, we will have the 21st-century academic library.

This pseudorealistic portrait has little substance. Shifts in technology cannot be treated as isolated vectors, divorced from the human and social practices in which they are embedded. No matter how much pressure there is to conceive them as so, students are not customers, and academic libraries are not businesses. The explosion in digital resources reflects the rapid embracing of new tools and new techniques for knowledge production that have not followed the predicted paths. One need only read anything from the past 20 years of speculative writings on library and technology futures to recognize how narrow our understanding of this process can be (and, one wonders, if this set of essays will fare any better). Yet we are not helpless. We can control our destiny in some, though definitely not all ways, if we conceive the challenges correctly.

Mission Alignment

The academic library is tied to the academic mission of the university. In contextual terms, we must recognize the shifts in scholarship practices that are occurring in our universities and research labs, and then seek to understand how the library functions appropriately in this new world where large data repositories become the norm for some disciplinary practices; where many students never visit a physical campus, let alone a library; where libraries assume part of the role of publishers; where tenure decisions are loosened from the documentary formats we have known for decades; and where special collections become indistinguishable from museums. As holders of the intellectual record, we need to reconsider how libraries interface with scholars working in remote teams sharing server space. With digital collections becoming boundary objects between academics, librarians, students, and designers in a manner that has no obvious historical parallel, the ability to engage in the most fundamental way with the mission of a university will define the importance of academic librarianship in the future.

Add to this the forms of information we deal with intellectually in academic life and the convergences we can witness between text, graphics, audio, and video forms. Libraries as collections of text are already challenged by the proliferation of mixed media. Data mined for meaning will give rise to dynamic representational forms of indeterminate temporal duration to be shared with distributed users, and museums, art galleries, and archives will increasingly lose the fixed walls of separation. Managing such information spaces will place emphases on interaction, organization, and curation in a manner that challenges existing practices. Success in this world is not measured by size of holdings or foot traffic, and control cannot be assumed through the provision of a catalog.

The academic library is anchored to an organizational form whose social contract and mission need not be radically altered by any technological advance. The future of academic libraries therefore will, I believe, be determined by the extent to which they amplify the mission of their host institutions and, ultimately, the mission of the university system at a national and international level. Since there is more than one type of academic institution, there will be more than one future for academic libraries. For those of us in research universities, the point can be made succinctly: libraries must enable and accelerate learning and discovery. Only by understanding this essential component of the university's goal can we steer a path through the ambiguities of the future.

Library as the Accelerator of Discovery

So what does it mean to enable or accelerate discovery? Ultimately, the acts of creation, learning, and discovery are fueled by the world in which we reside. The record of human knowledge ensures, at least in part, that humankind can make progress beyond the span of any one life. Newton stood on the shoulders of giants, but these giants left some clues. Broadly conceived, the modern academic library system is a repository of such clues as to the workings of our world and its contents. Such a purpose is noble and, to some extent, immune from shifts in technology, though one must accept both the threats and opportunities that such shifts might enable.

Among the threats we might expect are the economic costs of intellectual assets in a world where profit clearly follows control. When each individual is his or her own publisher, quality and, more likely, the ability to locate the quality among the dross, become vital. The tremendous opportunities involve much more than the clichéd 24/7 access to everything we are promised; they rest on the added value that comes from the power to mine vast corpora of data, the sharing of ideas independent of geography, and the genuine possibility of tailoring delivery in both form and rate to individual need and preference. It is not difficult to imagine how important a role an integrated system of academic libraries might play in both contexts, especially if we face up seriously to the thorny issue of assessing information quality.

As basic library functions shift from physical spaces to digital collections, the nature of reference work will adjust accordingly. Collection development, never an exact science, will be hugely important in an age of increasing data and a shortage of sophisticated filters. Where the catalog offered a point of entry to a bounded collection, the seamless access of digital resources requires us to design for more dynamic, unbounded, and nonlocal information. Clearly, there remains a need for more intelligent searching than is provided by Google, but we should not underestimate the power of technological advance to render current approaches to human guidance obsolete. The list continues. Take any attribute assumed core to the professional work of librarianship and you will find it altered on some level by the information world we now inhabit, bringing with it associated threats and opportunities.

Educating by Design

The ambiguities introduced by the shifts in information landscapes demand curricular responses from library and information science (LIS) programs to facilitate the development of the next generation of information professionals. The education of future information specialists for academic library work is also pressed by these changes in the academic landscape. In a rapidly changing technological environment, it is never enough to teach people to use these tools; the education process must enable students to adapt to new tools on an ongoing basis, and even to create their own tools. This certainly requires basic technological knowledge, but since much of what you can teach in a two-year master's degree program will be out of date by the time a graduate has joined the workforce, the most important educational function is the inculcation of a disposition toward technological innovation and a critical sense of how technology can serve and advance an organization's mission.

For all these changes, we must avoid the simple view of technological innovation and diffusion as one-directional. Technological shifts can operate in a refining manner, one that is not only revolutionary but that also returns us to the essentials of our craft. Librarianship is intellectual work, and the best practitioner's role is never determined solely by the technology (though generations of workers might have acted otherwise). Consequently, though media and forms of information might shift, the professional's role may thus be enhanced, especially where the shifts enable a new focus on the mission of the larger organization. Again, if our goal is to enable discovery, the emerging information infrastructure can place information professionals who fulfill this role at the center of activity.

It is possible to envisage a role for the information specialist as a true adjunct to the teaching mission by serving as a facilitator to students and researchers as they navigate information space. This is an established view of academic librarianship, but it is not always clear how best to interface the library with the classroom when libraries occupy physical spaces separate from the teaching and learning spaces in which students normally reside. I don't wish to diminish the value of rethinking the physical space of libraries and using computers and coffee to attract foot traffic, but the opportunity exists now to pull the collection into the temporal and physical environment of the classroom, or to shift the classroom from the lecture hall to the campus and beyond in ways that were never before possible.

On the research side, we have witnessed an explosion of digital resources in both the sciences and the humanities, and while the lone-scholar model will not disappear, the collaborative nature of research in many domains has enabled distributed teams of scholars to work together, sharing data, creating resources, and coauthoring without ever meeting. The outputs of these endeavors will not always find their resting place in established publishing venues, yet scholars will still require quality control, refereeing standards, tenure-and-promotion reviews, and grants. The process of enquiry will, in one sense, remain as it ever has, but the mechanisms involved, and the ability to engage and enable these scholarly activities, will require more than the provision of a physical space. When collaboration is truly loosened from colocation, we need to think differently about the wider system of academic libraries in which any one node is part of the greater intellectual resources of our world.

As well as the transformation of intellectual materials, we must recognize the attitudinal and cultural shifts that have occurred throughout the academy and our world in how information is viewed. Beyond mere access, faculty also view the intelligent management of information as part of their own working practices, bringing with them concerns with repositories, privacy, copyright, and migration across time and distance. Research publications now take many forms that tax previous understandings of process and protocol. Librarianship surely has a vital function in this.

Educating information professionals and librarians to thrive in this world is a question with which all forward-looking LIS programs are grappling. But in the spirit of refining our craft, the essential questions of information organization and navigation, quality assessment, and facilitation of discovery and learning remain. The opportunities we face now require, in my view, less a revolution in curricular type than in curricular form. The accredited master's program built on classroom lectures and term papers is ill-equipped to provide students with the type of skills they need.

There are no guaranteed right answers for many of the questions information professionals face. We must learn to accept this. Therefore, we need to educate practitioners who can tolerate these ambiguities and operate intelligently in the grey areas where intelligent trial and error may lead to the best outcomes. On the grounds that the best way to predict the future is to help design it, we must educate new professionals to be comfortable with technology, to be competent enough to participate in the design of new tools and services, and to have the necessary knowledge to evaluate their offerings in terms of how well they meet users' needs. Such an educational experience will involve technical skills that allow students to see beyond the surface of the digital environment, even if they never become proficient in programming; an understanding of the psychology of learning, research, and creativity so they can truly understand the users they serve; a sense of the legal and policy implications of information provisions; and a set of values that emphasize the vitality of the profession's legacies of access and stewardship.

I believe the incorporation of studio-based education in LIS would be an important step forward. Taking learners out of the "talking head"-dominated classroom environment into a new pedagogical model built on design and project experiences, at least as a complement to current forms, would offer budding professionals the chance to hone skills that will be essential in the coming years. This form of curricular innovation would tie education to professional practice in a manner more akin to design school than classic library school. Projects involving real clients would become a testing ground for ideas and potential solutions, providing the emerging professional with opportunities to hear from the field, work with an expert, and offer concrete responses. Coupled with a strong theoretical education in human information interactions, we would educate a class of professionals equipped to grapple with the ill-structured problems faced by academic libraries at this time.

Conclusion

Academic libraries will survive as long as there are universities. However, libraries cannot thrive without aligning their workings directly to the core mission of their host institutions. Augmenting the learning and research processes will require a deeper understanding of the underlying psychology and culture of these creative acts and experiences, coupled with an ability to experiment with and evaluate the effects of new tools. Libraries are not alone in this effort, and partnering with faculty in exploring new practices is necessary for real progress to occur.

The education of new academic librarians needs to be fostered through a more flexible, studio-based curriculum that builds the skills and knowledge required to participate intelligently in the changes affecting libraries. It will be vital to retain the values of the LIS field in each new generation of professionals while enhancing their abilities to accelerate human discovery. There is no one role for the future academic library, but there is one profession that addresses people's needs for information in a manner not distorted by concerns with profit or control. Our collective prosperity rests on our advancing this profession appropriately.

Groundskeepers, Gatekeepers, and Guides: How to Change Faculty Perceptions of Librarians and Ensure the Future of the Research Library

Daphnée Rentfrow

In November 2006 in Chicago, the Association of College and Research Libraries (ACRL) convened the Roundtable on Technology and Change in Academic Libraries to discuss the future of academic and research libraries. Leaders of the library profession discussed the impact of technology, the need for professional leadership to take on the challenges posed by new technologies, the characteristics new library professionals must possess to engage with the transformation of the profession, and the possibilities for the library's future relevance in society and higher education. The themes and conclusions of the roundtable were collected and presented in narrative form, and made available on the ACRL Web site.[1] Among the many valuable insights offered by the participants was the observation, worth reproducing here in its entirety, that academic and research libraries are facing a moment of opportunity that, if seized and capitalized upon, can place the library at the center of the academic and scholarly mission of the university.

> The changes that are occurring—in technology, in research, teaching and learning—have created a very different context for the missions of academic and research libraries. This evolving context can afford a moment of opportunity if libraries and librarians can respond to change in proactive and visionary ways. There are diverse and unmet needs now arising within the academy—many of which closely align with the traditional self-definitions of academic and research libraries. To the extent that libraries and their leaders can reposition themselves to serve these evolving needs—which pertain in part to the centralized

Daphnée Rentfrow, a former CLIR Fellow, has a Ph.D. in Comparative Literature and is currently enrolled in the MLIS program at the University of Illinois, Urbana-Champaign.

[1] Gregory Wegner with Robert Zemsky. February 2007. Changing Roles of Academic and Research Libraries. Available at http://www.ala.org/ala/acrl/acrlissues/future/changingroles.cfm.

storage, description, and delivery of academic resources, and in part to the organization and support of scholarly communication within and across higher education institutions—libraries will emerge as even more central and vibrant resources for their institutions.

There is little to argue with here, and much to embrace and look forward to. I would like to add my perspective to the conclusions offered by the roundtable in an attempt to add some specificity to the conversation about how libraries and the profession can best position themselves in the new scholarly context of the early 21st century. In particular, I will focus on the importance of collaboration, "public relations," and professional training.

I have been asked to share my thoughts here because of my experiences and background. The feeling, apparently, is that as a scholar and teacher with a PhD in the humanities, a former Council on Library and Information Resources (CLIR) Fellow, a master of library and information science (MLIS) student, and a collaborator and consultant/writer on library issues, I have some unique perspective to offer. I like to think this is true. Certainly, as someone who "backed into" librarianship by way of a thematic research collection and who spent her CLIR postdoc year learning from leaders such as Deanna Marcum, Clifford Lynch, Don Waters, John Unsworth, and Susan Perry, I have had a unique and privileged introduction to the issues currently dominating the profession. But as someone who finished a doctoral program at an Ivy League university without once meeting my subject specialist (or even knowing what one was), as someone who taught courses without conferring with a librarian and who never encouraged undergraduates to do so, and worked on a thematic research collection without thinking of metadata or preservation until I had a panicked reason to, I also know fairly intimately the failings of, let's say, "public relations" and "outreach" that afflict academic and research libraries. My comments here will reflect that duality, or what I prefer to call "hybridity."

In the essay cited above, the authors write that

> Libraries and librarians have exemplified the ideal of a higher education that combines knowledge in depth with contextualized understanding of different fields and domains. The very fact of developing and managing a collection conferred on librarians a degree of authority and influence in shaping the process of research and education. Faculty have understood well-built collections as a means to enhance their own productivity in teaching and research.

This may have been true in the past, but I am fairly certain that most librarians in academic and research libraries today would not list "authority and influence" as their most recognizable traits. In fact, most librarians I know express frustration at the lack of understanding about their roles in the intellectual life of their institutions. New technologies of information, copying, and exchange have changed basic conceptions of knowledge production, management, and stewardship. In the process, the logic goes, "everyone" thinks they can find and interpret information and so no longer need an intermediary, and "everyone" thinks that "everything" is on the Web. While these generalizations, like all others, are gross simplifications, they reveal all we need to know about the general zeitgeist surrounding what was once the domain of trained librarians. This perceived democratization of access to our shared cultural texts has had the side effect of devaluing and demystifying the library profession. Unfortunately, in the "everyone" of the clichéd hyperbole we can include our most learned colleagues, university faculty.[2]

Faculty, to my mind, are the single greatest challenge facing the modern research and academic library. Without faculty support and understanding and without their regular collaboration with librarians, the research library will not survive. It may remain as an interesting museum piece or storage facility, but it will no longer be the heart of the institution.

But the opposite is also true: If we can get faculty and scholars to be willing and eager collaborators with librarians in their course development, teaching, and research, then we will have guaranteed the active and irreplaceable role of the library in higher education, no matter how many books are digitized or how much shelf space is given over to cafés.

I am not alone in thinking that attention to faculty is of primary importance. The September/October 2007 issue of *EDUCAUSE Review* was dedicated to that premise. Entitled "Back to School: It's All About the Faculty," it included the title article and others, like "Wikis and Podcasts and Blogs! Oh, My! What Is a Faculty Member Supposed to Do?" and "Faculty 2.0." The assumption was, correctly, that reaching faculty and helping them understand why and when they require the collaborative energies of information technology (IT) specialists is key to advancing the goals of higher education and the IT profession. The same is true for libraries.

Unfortunately, non-librarian faculty members often do not appreciate the need for collaboration with librarians, nor do they see the library in more than traditional terms. The seismic changes that have affected librarianship and the ways in which the profession can and should be intimately involved with advanced research and undergraduate education have, for the most part, not changed how scholars think of the library. Faculty, at least in the humanities, have misconceptions about the modern research library in part because literary theory and cultural studies theory have made it unnecessary to include discussions of editions and bibliographic theory in a literature course. Once theory "killed" the "author" and made texts into contexts, there was little reason to concentrate on topics like the

2 By "faculty," I mean non-librarian teaching faculty and scholars. While some universities offer librarians faculty status, while some librarians consider themselves members of the faculty, and while some librarians have Ph.D. degrees, anecdotal evidence shows that students, parents, faculty, and even university administrators rarely consider libraries to be "real" faculty, or even intellectual peers. This problem of image is one of the biggest challenges facing the profession.

history of the book, editions, primary sources, and archival research. Alternately, other scholars in the humanities have developed an entirely new field around these questions, and yet librarians again have rarely been key players in the field. Humanities scholars who were early advocates for and scholars of computing developed their interests in small networks of subspecialists that quickly became coteries whose scholarship and publications often excluded the non-initiate. The field remained (and, arguably, remains) small and limited in such a way that librarians are often as excluded from the field, as are traditional humanists who have not "caught on" to the intellectual value or labor represented by, for example, text encoding or thematic research collections. Sadly, the exclusion of librarians in both undergraduate course development and advanced scholarship has created a climate in which librarians find themselves struggling to explain their role in research and teaching even to university administrators.3

Consider the following example. In September 2005, *The Chronicle of Higher Education* online published two position papers on whether or not academic librarians should receive tenure, and then opened a forum for debate of the issue. One commenter, identified as "senior prof," wrote in the forum that "[T]enure is for those who teach. [L]ibrarians are nothing more than part of the university staff. Is anyone out there recommending tenure for other staff such as office secretaries or the groundskeepers?" Putting aside the issue of tenure, this comment highlights the problem facing the profession as it begins to change its role in the landscape of the modern academic and research library. The sweeping changes in technology, information management and distribution, preservation, and discoverability have already affected the way research is conducted and shared, and these changes will only accelerate in the coming decades. Heated discussions are already taking place in the academy concerning which paradigms will most likely influence future hiring and promotion criteria. Consider the Modern Language Association (MLA) Task Force on Evaluating Scholarship for Tenure and Promotion, which has recommended that the humanities need to move away from the "tyranny of the monograph" and to recognize the legitimacy of new scholarship produced in new media.4

Just as future faculty hires will be expected to integrate new technologies and interdisciplinary strategies into their teaching and research agendas, and just as changes in hiring and promotion will

---

3 Several of my recent conversations and interviews with library directors have touched on this very topic; namely, that university provosts and presidents often express surprise when the library petitions for a larger budget or more staff, or argues for more involvement in curricular issues. There have even been anecdotes of administrators asking, with a straight face, "Isn't everything on the Web?" While these stories are mostly apocryphal, they capture the general sense of frustration library leaders are experiencing.

4 Stanton, Domna C., et al. 2007. Report of the MLA Taskforce on Evaluating Scholarship for Tenure and Promotion. Pp. 9-71 in *Profession*, edited by Rosemary G. Feal. New York: The Modern Language Association of America. The report also includes recommendations for evaluating scholarship in and about new media and on evaluating collaboration and collaborative authorship in the humanities.

begin to reflect these changes, academic research librarians will be tasked with accommodating new models of scholarship, promotion, and collaboration at the institutional, national, and even international levels. Their own hiring and promotion practices should similarly change to accommodate these models. This will require a shift in the conception and structure of the professional training librarians receive—one that will constitute an escalation in "applied" librarianship with a concurrent understanding of the new rigors of scholarship and the shifting boundaries of disciplinary inquiry. Simply put, the professional degree that has been the entry ticket into librarianship must place greater emphasis on how library professionals will meet the challenges of working closely with scholars and faculty while still ensuring the integrity, viability, dependability, and usability of the library itself.

The most important area needing development, in my experience, is the professional training librarians receive. This is a touchy subject, and I am sure what I have to say here will offend some readers. Nevertheless, I believe it needs to be said. As someone with a PhD who recently completed her MLIS degree at the top-rated library school in the country, I clearly believe there is value in the library degree. But as someone with a master's and a PhD in the humanities, I can also say that my library education was not as rigorous as my other graduate training—there is no comparison. And my point is that there shouldn't be. Both tracks and both degrees are good for what they are good for. That is to say, the PhD trained me in scholarship, research skills, writing, and teaching. The MLIS is training me in general areas of librarianship and information management.[5] Having experienced both, I can understand why a scholar would bristle to be told that a librarian has an equal understanding of the rigors of scholarship and full course-load teaching. But I also understand that the average faculty member is largely ignorant of the changes that have affected modern librarianship in recent decades and the ways these changes (should) affect scholarship and teaching. For these reasons, I have often been disappointed when the professor in one of my library courses makes a comment about inept and clueless humanities faculty members, and then enjoys a laugh with students, rather than addressing why there is a disconnect and encouraging discussion on how to bridge it. I have heard professors who have not earned a degree in the humanities talk about the needs and habits of humanists, focusing in particular on their lack of interest in the digital form, completely omitting conversations about digital humanities. I have been assigned readings that perpetuate the idea of faculty as "problem patrons," yet offered no readings on collaborative initiatives or successful models of outreach to redress the problem. In other areas, I have been frustrated that conversations about digital humanities and thematic research collections have been

---

[5] I purposely pursued a broad and generalized course of study rather than a focused one in, say, digital librarianship. My goal in attending library school was to see the ways in which the profession was defined and taught through immersion in coursework, and I wanted a range of perspectives.

left, for the most part, to advanced classes for those concentrating on digital librarianship. The topics should be addressed in any class with students possibly interested in working in a research library. I have been saddened that only a few professors encourage students to write about "big ideas" (that is, the cultural history of the book, cultural memory, the politics of preservation, representations of librarians, scholarship in the digital age) and instead have heard several professors and librarians assure LIS students that publishing in the profession is "easy" and that "most anything" can get published. If this is the talk in library schools and among librarians, can we really be upset or shocked when faculty feel collaboration with librarians is unnecessary?

On the other hand, I have been impressed with the quality of intellectual debate in most of my classes, the depth and breadth of courses, and my exchanges with other students. I have learned more than I had anticipated and while I learned just as much, if not more, as a CLIR Fellow, I am pleased with my decision to pursue the degree. In general, however, I feel that the curriculum of our library schools as it applies to academic librarianship, specifically in the humanities, needs to change if we hope to train new librarians who will be up to the challenges of working closely with scholars and faculty. One can envision these curricular changes in different ways, and another article would be the place to describe them. I am convinced, however, that the training and experience of humanities PhDs, coupled with intense introduction to librarianship through an apprenticeship or fellowship program, is one way to satisfy what will soon be a pressing need in the profession.

In addition to curricular changes, I see some professional ones that should be considered. They include the following:
- Libraries should be open to hiring more individuals who do not have the ML(I)S degree but who come with scholarly skills and teaching experience that make up for the lack of the professional degree.
- The profession should find creative ways to design new staff positions that serve as full-time liaisons linking the library and course development, especially in the area of digital resource use.
- Librarians should demand more of their professional publications and should publish widely and often on intellectual and philosophical issues facing the profession and scholarly communication and research in general, publish in journals outside the profession, and contribute to conferences outside the profession.
- Librarians should talk with each other across institutions and with the faculty who "get it" about how to persuade more faculty to collaborate on courses and curricular issues and should be willing to try both new approaches and approaches that failed in the past but that may now find footing.
- Institutions should promote successes more vocally—relying on word of mouth of one satisfied faculty member cannot have the same effect as would a smartly engineered marketing campaign.
- Libraries should demand more of university administrators—if

the library does not get enough respect, it must find ways to command it.

- Librarians should work with departments and teaching centers to nurture the idea that the library is a part of all teaching initiatives on campus.

None of these suggestions is new, and most are in practice—in some way, shape, or form—at academic and research libraries across the country. They are offered here as an affirmation and a reminder that the power to change perceptions of the profession rests within the profession. Change must take place in all areas, from training to hiring practices to professional development and rewards to institutional programs, but it must take place with vision and consistency.

Luckily, some models are available to us. For example, the hiring of non-MLIS scholars to positions of leadership in library schools demonstrates a change in attitude about the collaboration between librarians and scholars—digital humanists in particular. Similarly, having scholars in related fields teach in a library science program helps develop a sense of mutual respect and a model of collaboration that will shape how future academic librarians think about scholarship and their profession. This is especially true in the digital humanities. If librarians are to convince faculty that they are their intellectual equals, then the degree cannot be simply a vocational one. What is needed for the research library of the future are librarian-scholars prepared and trained by degree programs that require rigorous scholarship, publication, and teaching as part of the training. One model might be a separate track designed specifically for academic librarians. What matters is that we will need scholars with PhDs and experience in library-related issues as much as we will need degree-holding librarians with additional research experience. Either degree alone—PhD or MLIS—will not suffice to meet the needs of faculty, scholars, and students in the next decades.[6] The successful research library of the future will have a staff composed of many types of librarians, and even some who go by a different professional moniker. Scholars with PhDs, MLIS-holding librarians, "hybrids" with both degrees, and others with neither degree will all have a role to play. Some will be housed in the library, some in academic departments, and some in teaching centers. Some will be unmoored consultants. The most successful (and healthiest) libraries, I predict, will be those in which the differences are not cause for territorialism or professional angst but rather are a source of mutual respect and collaboration.

Asked to determine 10 assumptions about the future that would have a significant impact on academic libraries and librarians, an

---

6 Todd Gilman and Thea Lindquist recently published the results of their survey of librarians working in academic and research libraries who hold doctoral degrees in a discipline other than LIS. Their essay, and a planned follow-up essay on the professional tracks available to PhD-holding librarians, should prove useful to the conversation on the future of the research library. See "Academic/ Research Librarians with Subject Doctorates: Data and Trends 1965–2006." *portal: Libraries and the Academy* 8(1) (January 2008): 31-52.

ACRL research committee chose the following assumptions as their top two:

1. *There will be an increased emphasis on digitizing collections, preserving digital archives, and improving methods of data storage and retrieval.* Academic libraries have an opportunity to make their unique collections available to the world in unprecedented ways. In fact, the digitization of unique print collections may emerge as one of the primary missions of academic libraries in the 21st century. Librarians should collaborate with disciplinary colleagues in the curation of data as part of the research process.

2. *The skill set for librarians will continue to evolve in response to the needs and expectations of the changing populations (students and faculty) that they serve.* Changes in skill sets among library professionals are well under way. Entry-level salaries are increasing, due in part to the increased expectations of a new generation of professionals who have other career options. The aging of the profession can be viewed as having a number of positive benefits, for as retirements increase, new opportunities will open for a new generation of MLS librarians and other allied professionals. Libraries that are open to creating new career paths within their organizations are in an optimal position to embrace the future.[7]

Digitization, collaboration with disciplinary colleagues, new skills for the librarian, open-minded hiring practices—these are the issues that must take priority in the profession if it is to remain relevant. If successfully managed, all will result in renewed respect for the profession, increased opportunities for collaboration, and increased institutional support.

The research library safeguards those materials that make it possible for scholars to do their work and for students to explore their own interests and to develop their curiosity. It is a space of intellectual exchange—with others, with one's self, and with the thinkers and texts of the past. It is the home base of highly trained professionals dedicated to harnessing, guiding, preserving, and complementing the knowledge produced by the scholars, teachers, and students who use the collection. Reaching the faculty and scholars who are served by academic and research libraries must be the priority for the library profession if we want to meet the challenges of the 21st century. The creation, preservation, dissemination, and stewardship of knowledge is the library's core mission. By reaching out to and collaborating with faculty and converting them to the belief that librarians are central to their own research and teaching, the research library will come to once again house, both literally and symbolically, the heart of the university and to represent, in practice and vision, the very best of the ideals of the liberal arts.

---

7 Mullins, James L., Frank R. Allen, and Jon R. Hufford. 2007. Top Ten Assumptions for the Future of Academic Libraries and Librarians: A Report from the ACRL Research Committee. *C&RL News* 68(4). Available at http://www.ala.org/ala/acrl/acrlpubs/crlnews/backissues2007/april07/tenassumptions.cfm. Accessed December 4, 2007.

Leveraging Digital Technologies in Service to Culture and Society: The Role of Libraries as Collaborators

Lee L. Zia[1]

Approximately a decade and a half has passed since the phrase "World Wide Web" and its enabling technology burst onto the scene. During that time stunning increases in communication and computational capabilities, coupled with equally dramatic decreases in cost, have produced networked information technology devices that have changed and continue to change fundamentally the relationship between people and knowledge.

This same period has also witnessed the evolution of the Internet from a pure research and development environment to one that pundits assert reflects the "commoditization of the Internet." Closely associated with this growth in the commercial Internet has been the emergence of participatory capabilities for individuals that find their most recent expression in the rise of social networking trends, services, and community formation. This democratization of access to data and information has altered not just the "where" and "when" of learning, but increasingly the "how" and "by whom" that authority or certification of expertise is obtained or granted.

These changes challenge many concepts and traditions: the idea of the original, authoritative source, the fate of books, the role of libraries, the place of formal institutions of learning, the nature of discourse, and, of course, "old" business models—all subject to various manifestations of the tension between atoms and bits, as Negroponte termed it in "Being Digital." Do libraries need survival skills? Yes, but society and culture need survival skills even more, and libraries will survive if they are relevant to this larger task. To navigate successfully the circumstances produced by the amazing explosion of access to unfiltered data and the changing relationship of people to

Lee L. Zia is Lead Program Director of the National Science Digital Library Program at the National Science Foundation.

[1] The views expressed in this essay are entirely those of the author and do not represent official policy of the National Science Foundation.

knowledge, the library, with its rich traditions of attention to stewardship, preservation, quality, and providing at least a proxy for the certification of authority, will play an important role in collaboration with its constituencies: end users and content providers.

The next section offers examples of the way in which libraries have participated in interesting collaborations to grapple with the changes brought by the digital era. The particular perspective taken is from the science, technology, engineering, and mathematics (STEM) educational enterprise, with all examples drawn from projects funded under the National Science Foundation's (NSF) National Science Digital Library Program (NSDL). Two "meta-themes" reflected in this collective set of projects are the integration of research and education missions, and the blurring of formal and informal learning opportunities.

Examples From the NSDL Program

During the mid- to late-1990s, NSF provided leadership and primary funding for the Digital Libraries Initiative—Phase 1 and Phase 2, a multiagency digital library research program. Building on that early work, the NSDL program began (and continues) to support the establishment of a national digital library for science education that constitutes an online network of learning environments and resources for STEM education at all levels, in both formal and informal settings. A key assumption of the program from its inception was that the effort should take a distributed-development approach, reflecting the underlying distributed nature of the Web. From a practical perspective, the decision to adopt a distributed approach also reflected the fact that underlying Web technology was constantly changing and improving, thus the effort should attempt to be as open and flexible as possible without making a single centralized investment that might lead to decisions that would prematurely lock the overall development into a narrow path.

This approach also enabled learners and other end-users to bring their needs more explicitly to the table since one of the advantages of the digital era has been to enable much more participation by end-users of technology in its actual design and deployment. In fact the theme of distributed development has found a natural extension to the project level, in that many NSDL projects have typically featured collaboration among multiple partners representing a number of broad areas: (1) academic, disciplinary expertise typically in the form of faculty leaders of educational innovations; (2) computer science/digital library researchers and information science researchers; (3) traditional library personnel or media specialists (a term increasingly used in the K–12 sector); and (4) more recently, the informal learning sector (e.g., museums and science centers).

The examples that follow illustrate several common ingredients. Foremost is the existence of an interesting problem or challenge whose form in the context of educational digital libraries has an applied nature to it. There is also mutual self-interest on the part of collaborators, a sense that they are engaged in shared problem solving. All parties bring expertise to contribute, and they find value or benefit in what they learn and take away from the effort. The successful collaborations have also developed a genuine sense of collegiality that grows from having a collective sense of purpose. In many ways this is a "meta-feature" that characterizes the way in which the various NSDL projects have worked with one another. Finally, one cannot ignore the role that external funding plays in catalyzing project work that crosses administrative and disciplinary boundaries; while not sufficient it is often necessary. Challenges remain, of course, and the final section of this essay provides commentary on a number of these.

The examples of projects below focus on three themes: (1) metadata standards development with particular application to the alignment of educational resources to national and state science and mathematics standards; (2) integration of digital library resources and frameworks with the infrastructure and processes of the traditional (physical) library; and (3) development and deployment of services. These themes reflect not just areas of interest but also in some sense an evolutionary record of how the digital library field has matured—a natural progression as both underlying technologies and standards have developed. (Award numbers are given with the first two digits reflecting the fiscal year chronology of the cited project.)

Before turning to the examples, it is important to note that none of the NSDL effort has taken place in a vacuum. The larger arena in which all the projects have operated has benefited from and been informed enormously by the advocacy and leadership of the Council on Library and Information Resources (CLIR), the Coalition of Networked Information (CNI), and the Digital Library Federation (DLF), to name but a few organizations. Additionally, much support to the field and leadership has come through projects funded by the Institute for Museum and Library Services (IMLS) and The Andrew W. Mellon Foundation.

Metadata Standards Development and Assignment

Attention in many early NSDL projects centered on the promotion of metadata standards for the description of educational resources. As many a wag has noted, "The great thing about standards is that there are so many to choose from!" Humor aside, early NSDL projects did in fact grow from the work of the Dublin Core effort (an early collaboration of individuals and institutions that married library expertise with computer science expertise) and other standards efforts such as the Learning Object Metadata work of the Institute of Electrical and Electronics Engineers (IEEE). Acknowledging the importance of enhancing interoperability among different digital library approaches, NSDL projects promoted collectively the adoption of at least minimal metadata standards and cross-walking methods. Toward this end, the NSDL program introduced language in its early calls for proposals that strongly urged projects to adhere at a minimum to the

Dublin Core metadata standards so as to promote metadata sharing and federation of collections. This step was seen as a minimally necessary condition to ensure that the results of many diverse cataloging efforts could be leveraged to enable search and discovery over a much larger universe of resources than those identified by a single collection. Without such sharing, an individual collection would risk painting itself into an electronic corner of the Web. The introduction of the Open Archives Initiative's protocols for metadata harvesting (OAI-PMH) also aided this step to raise the standards bar.

Against this broad backdrop of attention to the importance of metadata and in recognition of the labor-intensive nature of human cataloging, a collaboration headed by researchers at the University of Washington's Information School and university library colleagues (NSF-0121717) began to investigate automated processes to complement human effort. The team also involved the Syracuse University Center for Natural Language Processing and practitioners from Mid-continent Research for Education and Learning (McREL), a nonprofit organization with roots as a U.S. Department of Education regional education laboratory. To automatically assign content standards and other benchmarks to educational resources in the collections of NSDL, the project has developed a natural language processing tool (StandardConnection). The standards and benchmarks come from the McREL Compendium of Standards and Benchmarks and represent both state and national science education standards. Supplementing general descriptive metadata, the content standards metadata make it possible for a teacher in any state to use the NSDL to locate teaching resources for helping students achieve a particular competency set by the state. The overall process involves training the tool on a set of educational resources, cultivating a deep understanding of human cognitive processes involved in manual assignment of content standard metadata tags, iteratively adjusting the tool until reliable tagging is produced, and employing teacher-experts to analyze the quality of the tool's mappings of resources to standards and benchmarks during an evaluative phase.

Building on this research effort, an implementation project led by Diekema and others at Syracuse (NSF-0435339) has focused on improving the ability of teachers to locate science and mathematics resources that support their standards-based instruction, no matter what state they are in or where a resource was developed. Two services are currently available for NSDL collection providers. The first is a Computer-Assisted Standard Assignment recommender tool that suggests to a human cataloger one to five of the most relevant national content standards appropriate for a learning resource. The cataloger accepts, edits, or rejects these suggestions, and the tool adds them to the resource's metadata records. The system learns from vetted assignments in order to inform future standards recommendations for increased accuracy. The second service is a methodology and tool that crosswalks between math and science state standards and their national counterparts. The resulting automated mapping between state and national standards allows the national standards to function as an "exchange" standard. NSDL's search capabilities incorporate this mapping facility so that teachers can search for resources using either their home-state standards or the national standards. Furthermore, educational resources may be easily shared from anywhere in the country once a translation between state standards is facilitated.

A third example in this set involves a collaboration led by library staff at Cornell University (Hillman et al., see NSF-0532854). The team is developing and deploying a metadata registry service to complement the NSDL Data Repository. The registry is based on the open-source Dublin Core Metadata Initiative (DCMI) Registry application and enables multiple diverse collection providers and other NSDL projects to identify, declare, and publish their metadata schemas (element/property sets) and schemes (controlled vocabularies). The project provides support for registration of schemes and schemas for use by human and machine agents, as well as support for the machine mapping of relationships among terms and concepts in those schemes (semantic mappings) and schemas (crosswalks). Generalization of registry software enables implementations beyond centrally controlled metadata schemas, thus placing the distribution of appropriate control and management in the hands of vocabulary creators and maintainers. In turn this offers the potential to overcome economic and legal barriers that have prevented the anticipated growth of registries and distributed registry networks.

Integrating Physical and Digital Traditions

A second area of exploration for NSDL projects has been in how to connect the digital with the physical world. Here collaboration plays an important role not so much with respect to individual implementations that must necessarily reflect local circumstances, but in terms of sharing of experiences that can allow the identification of common principles and best practices.

In the project "Adding Value to the NSDL by Integrating it into Academic Libraries: A Business Proposition and a Service Enhancement" (NSF-0333710), Greenstein and others working across the University of California (UC) system conducted market research to evaluate what content and services the NSDL needs to offer to attract and thus support itself at least in part with subscriptions paid by academic libraries. A second strand of activity developed a prototype service that integrates NSDL into the foundational science collections managed by various libraries within the UC system. The service includes tools that enable libraries to create views of their integrated science collections customized to the needs of different patrons. While mainly a proof-of-concept effort, this aspect of the project promises to inform the modifications that the NSDL and its collection providers may need to make to their technical architectures to enable them to better support integration into academic library collections. The libraries within the larger UC system exhibit highly diverse technical environments and thus have offered an excellent testbed setting for service deployment and evaluation representative of the heterogeneous technical environments that characterize academic libraries in general.

A second project has considered this integration challenge at a single institutional or local level. In "Integrating Digital Libraries and Traditional Libraries: A Model for Sustaining NSDL Collections" (NSF-0333628), Ward led a team at the University of North Carolina at Wilmington (UNC-Wilmington) to investigate the issues involved when integrating an existing NSDL collection, the iLumina digital repository, with a traditional research library, the Randall Library at UNC-Wilmington. Lessons from this project offer guidance for sustaining the many digital collections that reside at institutions of higher education. As part of this effort, the project sought to automate the conversion of Instructional Management Systems (IMS) metadata to MARC data records through an implementation of XML harvester software to transform IMS metadata compiled in the iLumina digital collection directly into MARC data records used in the Randall Library catalog. As iLumina resources are listed within the Randall Library catalog, they become shareable with the OCLC WorldCat database, thus substantially increasing the accessibility of the digital resources originally known only to the local digital repository.

Digital Library Service Frameworks

A third area where NSDL projects have made inroads is in the development of frameworks for service creation and deployment. This area of effort complements the second set of projects described above. For example, in the OCKHAM project (see NSF-0333497), Frumkin at Oregon State, along with collaborators in the University Library at Emory and computer scientists at Virginia Polytechnic Institute, have focused on developing networked middleware to facilitate and expand access to the content and services of the NSDL through the existing national infrastructure of traditional libraries and their service programs. Additionally, the team has created a reference model for integrating the NSDL into traditional library services; evaluating the utility, usage, and impacts of the local library tested services on the participating campus communities through Web log analysis, focus groups, and usability studies; and disseminating results and facilitating growth of the network among an expanding group of institutional partners. By stimulating an extensible framework for networked peer-to-peer interoperation among the NSDL and traditional libraries, this project is also advancing the dialog between librarians and researchers.

Mischo and others at the University of Illinois head a second, more recent project of this type (see NSF-0734992). This team is developing and implementing a set of metasearch gateway services for the distributed NSDL community that use broadcast search technologies to provide access to selected scientific and engineering publisher full-text repositories, abstracting and indexing services, university institutional repositories, open-access full-text journal and report sites, and the efforts of the NSDL Pathways projects. As a component of the NSDL core integration services, the gateways provide custom federated search access to critical distributed information resources that support the instructional and research needs of middle school, high school, undergraduate, and graduate students as well as faculty. Standards-based frameworks are in use such as the NISO MXG (Metasearch XML Gateway) framework, the OpenSearch 1.1 standard, and the Open Archives Initiative protocols for metadata harvesting (OAI-PMH) and for object reuse and exchange (OAI-ORE). Furthermore, the project features a collaboration of information science researchers with personnel from the DLF Aquifer project and an international component involving two Joint Information Systems Committee (JISC)-funded initiatives in the United Kingdom: the PerX project at Heriot-Watt University and the CREE project headquartered at the University of Hull. The latter connections speak to the broader impacts of this project on the global educational digital libraries environment.

A final example illustrates the emergence of utility-like application services. Late in summer 2007, NSDL initiated a collaboration with the Colorado Alliance of Research Libraries (CARL) through which CARL has adopted the NSDL Data Repository and its Fedora-based technology platform to provide distributed collection management for its 11 member institutions. This work is just now under way, and is beginning with the creation, storage, management, and delivery of very large image collections from the member libraries. A key public benefit of the project is that it will enable these resources to be accessible to all school districts across Colorado and Wyoming. This initial effort points the way toward the provision of more extensive repository services for the text, image, and video resources of the alliance. As more libraries and cultural heritage institutions begin to consider digital repositories, this collaboration presents a model for new NSDL partnerships. This example, like the previous two examples in this section, illustrate how libraries can, and perhaps ultimately must, participate in an effort that is beyond what each can take on individually.

Ongoing Challenges

As the previous examples show, research libraries have played an important, and often leading, role in projects that have charted new directions in managing data and information in the digital age, and pointed the way toward the development of new digital library services. Such work could not have been undertaken without the involvement of a diverse set of principal investigators, and it has been gratifying to witness the collaboration among units on campuses that previously did not interact much. Indeed, just bringing such groups together has been a notable achievement.

Many challenges remain if the library and scholarly community are to exercise leadership in determining how to leverage the advantages of digital technologies for the benefit of culture and society.

Chief among them are the following:

- Engaging the broader library community in implementing leading-edge advances such as those described above and others resulting from programs offered by IMLS and private funders such as the Mellon Foundation. More than just a matter of disseminating information about these advances, this broader engagement will require systematic and systemic effort to help different audiences learn a new language, with faculty needing to understand issues of librarianship and librarians growing to appreciate faculty roles. Of particular interest is the challenge these changing roles will place on the future structure and content of graduate and professional school programs.

- Supporting continued educational-content development and innovation that can be made available through locally maintained digital repositories and shared through a broad network of contributing providers. While producers have primarily been from the higher education community, the rapidly evolving capabilities for reusing and re-forming content are broadening participation in this activity quickly. Key issues will continue to revolve around questions such as authenticity, certification of expertise, and mechanisms and practices for attribution of creation.

- Evaluating the educational impact of the increased access to resources and data that digital libraries make possible; developing metrics to capture the degree of reuse, repurposing, or repackaging of digital material; and assessing the value of such activities.

- Supporting continued research efforts in the management, manipulation, and storage of large heterogeneous data sets; and the development of new tools, methodologies, processes, and services to meet the educational and other scholarly needs of learners.

- Developing increased understanding and satisfaction of end-user needs that move beyond pure searching for factual "data" to more-nuanced, semantically imbued sense making. Here the push toward increased customization must be balanced against privacy concerns.

Perhaps the greatest need is to create and sustain the ability to address the multiple challenges identified above. One possibility is to place responsibility in the hands of a nonprofit organization to provide leadership for the science education and scholarly community to meet these challenges. In this vision, the library would provide a natural voice through which to express an institution's priorities. And its assets, not only in the form of an institutional repository and services, but more importantly its human resources, would in effect serve as a currency to contribute to the larger national (if not international) organization. Within such a larger organization, the preservation of institutional branding and the companion issue of ownership would present an ongoing challenge. However, the NSDL projects have shown that mutual self-interest and a sense of shared problem solving can lead to significant collaborations among different units on campuses. Furthermore, as the examples illustrate, interinstitutional collaborations have formed naturally, transcending institutional identity. Indeed, the community of NSDL projects has self-organized into multiple standing committees and workgroups to tackle collectively numerous tasks including policy development in areas such as: collection development, privacy, copyright, metadata standards and guidelines, and metadata sharing. In addition, collaboratively developed services such as those described above have been created.[2]

How might such a virtual organization come into being? One model finds its inspiration in the creation of NSFnet, which is currently celebrating its 20th anniversary. Specifically, it is fitting to envision an analog to the NSFnet "connectivity" program in which educational institutions would receive initial support to join a (virtual) organization as a member institution for several years. However, grants would not be for physical connectivity, but rather

- to build capacity to make locally developed educational resources and services—institutional repositories—available to a wider audience via the NSDL (gaining access in return to the larger collective body of resources and services), and
- to support local teacher/faculty development activities to engage educators in how to make use of the new capabilities of NSDL and the resources to which it provides access.

Continued membership would fall on the institution. A relatively modest annual fee, multiplied across interested institutions of higher education and local school districts, would generate a significant source of *self-sustaining* revenue.[3] As the network effect took hold—with the value of the network increasing as more members join—such a strategy would enable NSF and other funders to transition support for this facility to a community-based mechanism.

[2] For more details, see http://nsdl.org/resources_for/library_builders/nsdlgroups.php, and a related link at http://nsdl.org/resources_for/library_builders/tools.php?pager=tools.

[3] There are about 4,000 higher education institutions and about 16,000 local school districts in the United States. An average $10,000/year fee would permit a $200M/year operating budget. The annual fee could be scaled to reflect attributes such as institution size, population, and other socioeconomic factors. The fee could be thought of as an ongoing subscription (see http://www.dlib.org/dlib/march01/zia/03zia.html and the section on Sustainability). Museums and public libraries would also be able to subscribe.